CLASSIC
HOT RODS

Bo Bertilsson

MBI Publishing Company

Acknowledgments

Among the people who made this book possible, I wish to thank my old friend Tony Thacker for help with pictures and good connections, and Greg Sharp and Michael Dobrin for being so kind and letting me use some of their historic pictures. Geoff Carter and my old friends Kjell Gustavsson and Erik Hansson contributed pictures. I also wish to thank Pete Chapouris, Jim Jacobs, Bruce Meyer, Thom Taylor, Tom Vogele, Joe Reath, and Stig Sjöberg.

—Bo Bertilsson

First published in 1999 by MBI Publishing Company, 729 Prospect Avenue, PO Box 1, Osceola, WI 54020-0001 USA

© Bo Bertilsson, 1999

MBI Publishing Company books are also available at discounts in bulk quantity for industrial or sales-promotional use. For details write to Special Sales Manager at Motorbooks International Wholesalers & Distributors, 729 Prospect Avenue, PO Box 1, Osceola, WI 54020-0001 USA.

Library of Congress Cataloging-in-Publication Data

Bertilsson, Bo.
    Classic hot rods/Bo Bertilsson.
        p. cm.
    Includes index.
    ISBN 0-7603-0721-0 (pbk.: alk. paper)
    1. Hot rods. I. Title.
TL236.3.B47   1999
629.228'6—dc21   99-34068

On the front cover: The lines on this beautiful, black roadster define the most classic hot rod style you can find. Doane Spencer started to build his roadster in 1937 but didn't finish it until after he came back from World War II. Sometime in the 1950s, Spencer sold the car in parts to *Rod & Custom* editor Lynn Wineland. In turn, Wineland sold the unfinished car in 1969 to Neal East who put the flathead back in it. He drove it for many years before collector Bruce Meyer bought the historic car. Meyer had Pete Chapouris and crew restore the roadster to its original classic state. *Bo Bertilsson*

On the frontispiece: Ed Iskenderian built his first hot rod on an Essex frame that he bought in 1939 for fifteen bucks. Another sixty dollars and he was able to drop this 1932 Ford Flathead into it, but not before modifying it with a Winfield cam, a set of Maxi heads, plus a Thickstun manifold toppped with three 97 Stromberg carbs. Iskenderian later became famous for his own cams, known today worldwide as ""Isky Cams."

On the title page: This highboy is as classic as they come. Bill Burnham built the car about 20 years ago and based it on a '32 frame that was extended 4 inches and narrowed 2 inches at the firewall. The front end has an old dropped Merritt I-beam axle, '39 Ford spindles, and '40 Ford brakes with Buick drums. A split wishbone keeps the front end in place. The rear end is a 9-inch Ford that was narrowed a few inches before it was installed with a four-link setup and a pair of coil-over shocks.Most hot rodders will recognize this roadster. Burnham wrote a regular column for *Street Rodder* magazine, and a drawing of this car was at the top of each installment.

On the back cover: Two veritable hot rod classics: Ed "Isky" Iskenderian and the 1924 T-roadster he started to build in 1939. This rod debuted at El Mirage in 1942, turning in 120 miles per hour with Isky at the wheel. *Bo Bertilsson*

Designed by Todd Sauers

Printed in Hong Kong

Contents

Foreword

Yo brothers and sisters of hot rodding . . . Listen up! This is your favorite hot rod rebel of the '40s, Ed "Big Daddy" Roth, explaining why ya want this book and why it's so important to have it in your library.

So many of us old "Geezers" are dying off, that the real old days of hot rodding are getting lost and the truth is fading fast. You see, hot rodding was a full time activity in So Cal before '64. We raced, we cruised, and we had those innocent days of drive-ins and street races. Music was cool and surfing was the "in" thing to do. Even the music matched the times. It was great! If ya wanted parts or needed stuff, you had to make 'em.

Then things started tainting this great scene. In '64 wrenches and welding sets got turned in for guitars (I still can't believe it), and ducktails got turned into long, raunchy hair styles and earring-toting hippies, so that today we think in terms of half million–dollar turn-key roadsters. "Don't build it! Buy it!" Sad theme . . . Too bad! Close my eyes and die.

But wait. What wuz really up? What about future generations, and what will they think about us old-timers? Will they know the truth about those pioneers who got butchered at the races or the guys who did jail time for drag racing on the streets? That's where Bo's book fills the void. He's researched this book thoroughly. And although he is a native of Sweden, he has hung around L.A. long enough to capture the pride and esoteric values of the hot rod movement. Oh sure! He has thrown in a few of his favorite personal theories, but it's still the best out there.

Yes, hot rodding was started by those early pioneers who created the "look" of hot rodding. The fast engines and the raked bodies and the poodle-skirted "boogy woogying " chicks who made it happen. Not your Fonzie-styled Hollywood view of hot rodding . . . but the real story!

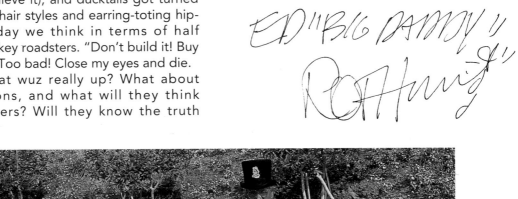

Ed "Big Daddy" Roth

Preface

It was in the mid-1950s, times were hard, and we lived in a very small one-bedroom apartment. To make a little extra money, dad had a second job at a magazine store, and one day he brought home an issue of *Hot Rod magazine* for me. It was several months old, but that didn't matter to me at all. I was in third grade and didn't even read English yet. Later, it was not hard for my English teacher to understand where my newfound interest in the language came from, because I wrapped my books with the covers from *Hot Rod magazine*. I wanted to be able to read at least the picture captions, so I decided to study the English books and pay attention to the teacher.

Soon I found out that other guys in school were also reading American car magazines at home. One of them, Anders, became my good friend. Some years later, Anders had told me that two local guys were working on some hot rods and custom cars. The first thing we did was go over there and check what was going on. They took us to a nearby barn where they were building their hot rods. One was a T-roadster with an Olds Rocket motor, and the other was a chopped-and soon-to-be-channeled '32 Ford coupe. The experience was overwhelming, and I went home feeling like I had kissed Marilyn Monroe. Those two hot rodders were Bo and Sven Sandberg. A few years later, in the mid-1960s, Bo organized the first hot rod show in Stockholm, possibly the first in Europe.

My interest in hot rods grew through the years, and in 1969 I talked my parents into lending me half the money I needed for a two-week trip to California. I wanted to see the Oakland Roadster Show and the street rod scene of Southern California.

Later, in Los Angeles, I just had to go and see Ed "Big Daddy" Roth at his Roth Studios in Maywood. Jake Jacobs worked at the studio at the time too, and he sold me a 1930 California license plate that is on my flathead T-roadster today. I didn't leave until late that night, after Ed had talked me into getting a good camera and shooting bike features for his *Choppers* magazine. By the time my first features had landed on his desk, he had sold the magazine, so he returned them. I didn't give up though, and I forwarded the features to the late Tom McMullen and his new *Street Chopper* magazine. He published them right away and wanted more. I was very proud and happy.

When those *Street Chopper* magazines hit the stands at the International Press store in Stockholm, something else happened. One day in 1971 I ran into Bo Sandberg again, and he said, "Don't send your stuff to America. You can work for my *Colorod* magazine instead." I began submitting articles to Bo, and by 1973 we were publishing nine issues a year of *Colorod*. At the time, it was the only hot rod, custom, and chopper magazine in Scandinavia. I became the editor of the magazine and later issued a couple of my own street rod and drag racing publications. On top of that, I was racing my own alcohol funny car on the European circuit.

Racing took too much of my time and money, so in 1985, after 10 years of the sport, I gave it up and decided to move to California. At that point I had given up the magazine and was working as a freelancer for other European magazines. I knew most of the editors of the European magazines, but once in America it took nearly five years to establish a good working relationship with some the enthusiast publications.

I am now also on the staff of Albinsson & Sjöberg Publishing, the largest automotive magazine publishing company in Scandinavia. That means more steady work, and I can work with my hobby full time for a few more years. Best of all, I was given the chance to do this book for MBI Publishing Company. I have many people to thank for pointing me in the right direction through the years, and I feel very lucky to be part of the West Coast hot rod scene. May you enjoy this book as much as I enjoyed writing it.

—*Bo Bertilsson*

This picture was taken by my late mentor, Bo Sandberg, as a Christmas card for *Colorod* magazine. Even if the editorial office never was this bad looking, the picture is a part of my hot rod background.

Chapter 1

HOW THE T-BUCKET WAS BORN

It was the October 1955 issue of *Hot Rod magazine*, with Norm Grabowski's T on the cover, that did it. When that magazine hit the newsstands, it changed the hot rod scene forever and defined the T-bucket's shape and form. There were many neat Model-T–based hot rods built before 1955, many of which were based on the early dirt track cars, but this was something new. Grabowski was the "creator of the bucket-T" but did not have any idea what he had started with his hot rod. The earlier cars were mostly modified, but Norm's T-bucket was built from scratch with highly modified parts, and it had a late-model overhead V-8. He started work on it in 1950 and completed it five years later.

In those days the cars were built with mostly old Ford parts, which were easy to find in the local scrap yards. Norm started with a Model-A frame, which was cut in the front. He made a new front cross-member out of a piece of tubing, with a bracket for the leaf spring, and used a tube axle from a 1937 Ford (60 HP V-8). That type of front axle became very popular on hot rods of the late '40s and early '50s, thanks to a little bit more drop

To run 11.25/125 miles per hour in a street roadster at the drag strip is not easy even today, and when Tommy Ivo did that in 1957 it must have been a shock to his opponents. The only things Ivo did to the car at the drag strip were to bolt in the roll cage and take the high windshield off. They ran the Buick motor either with the Hilborn fuel injection or six Stromberg 97s on a Weiand Drag Star manifold.

Norm Grabowski understood that the new overhead-valve motors were the future, so he used a nearly new 1952 Cad engine that was bored-out to 354 ci. A Winfield cam and a Horne manifold with four Stromberg 97 carburetors gave him some extra power. Constanza used the same recipe.

than the other stock axles. The dropped front axles were on the market in California at this time, but a '37 Ford axle was cheaper and looked much better in the front of a T. Rather than mount the front axle like on the stock '37 Ford, the clever Norm cut up a set of wishbones from a '40 Ford and turned them back-to-front, so the leaf spring was mounted behind the axle instead. That became known as the "suicide style," with the front axle hanging out in the front of the car. That way, the wheelbase became longer too (96 inches), and that gave the car better handling.

The rear end Norm used was out of a '41 Ford, and the drive shaft was shortened before the axle was mounted with a Model-A spring. The most common transmission in the hot rods of the '50s was the '39 Ford box, but if the motor was something more than a stock flathead, most hot rodders replaced the stock gears with a set of Lincoln Zephyr gears instead. As early as the mid-'50s, some companies had started to manufacture adapters to fit the new overhead valve V-8s to the

Franco Constanza brought back the Grabowski T in replica form, just like it was during the days when it was part of the TV series 77 Sunset Strip. It took Constanza 15 years to collect all the parts for the car, and a Model T steel body was used together with a shortened Model A pickup bed. Grabowski used a Model-A frame that he shortened in the rear about 6 inches, but lengthened in the front with the cut-off pieces. The frame rails are tapered, both front and rear; that's why he cut the frame. The high Model-A spring gave the car plenty of rake.

The interior was stitched in red leather, and the steering column came out of a '38 Chevy with a Bell steering wheel on top. The door on the right side was welded shut, and it was covered by the interior. The tall shifter of the '39 Ford trans is topped off with a skull.

Grabowski picked a '37 Ford front axle and reversed the spring-hangers, so the leaf-spring was mounted behind the axle instead. The axle is held in place by four Ford tie rods, the idea for which came from Sprint Cars. The half-moon-shaped brackets on the axle were bolted on for a tow-bar when it was time to go drag racing.

The rake was part of the "Kookie Car" style. Grabowski did not "Z" his frame in the rear, so he achieved the rake with the high Model-A rear spring on the '40 Ford rear end. The T-body was channeled 6 inches over the frame, and the windshield was made up from pieces of a 1922 Dodge windshield frame.

The Tommy Ivo T was restored by Ron Jones, and Ivo had to come to see the car and pose with it when it was completed. Jones had to replace the frame because restoring it was not possible. Ivo checked out Grabowski's T before he started building his own, so the chassis is nearly a copy of the Grabowski T. The only difference on the Ivo T is that he did a kick-up on his frame in the rear, to get a little less rake. Ivo raced a full-size Buick with a tuned motor before he built the T, and took the engine out of the Buick and dropped it in the T.

'39 Ford transmission. Norm Grabowski got hold of a 1952 Cadillac 354 engine, which he tuned up a bit, and later he mounted a 3-71 GMC blower on top of it. With the help of an adapter, he bolted the '39 Ford trans to the back of the Caddy motor.

The thing that gave Grabowski's T its real profile was not just the steel Ford '22 body, but the shortened Model-A pickup bed and the '22 Dodge leaned-back windshield. The rake in the car came from the straight Model-A frame and the high Model-A rear leaf spring. The 22-year-old Grabowski had created an original when he rolled his home-built hot rod out of the garage that day in 1955.

The *Hot Rod* magazine cover got things rolling. One day Norm had the drag racer and movie star, Tommy Ivo, over for a visit. But Ivo did not just want to take a closer look at the car; he wanted to measure everything on it, too. Ivo planned to build a car of his own, so he wanted all the proportions right before beginning. "TV Tommy" Ivo started a little bit differently, though, when he took the race Nailhead motor out of his full-size Buick and hooked that up to a '37 LaSalle transmission with the help of an Honest Charley adapter. The chassis build-up was nearly a copy of Grabowski's T, with a Model-A frame, a front suspension with a '37 tube axle, etc. The only big difference was that Ivo Z-ed his frame

in the rear, to get a little less rake, and mounted the rear spring on top of the rear end. To make the search for parts easier, he bought a wrecked '41 Ford. Some of those parts were the rear end, steering box and column, spindles, brakes, wishbones, and pedals with a master cylinder. Ivo also picked up some ideas that the sprint car racers were using, and made four Ford tie-rods into a four-link, to keep the front axle in place. Many years later, this kind of setup would become the standard of the hot rod business. Ivo found his steel body out in the desert, as a front half of a 1925 T Phaeton, and combined that with a shortened Model-A pickup bed. Both of the cars had reversed, painted Ford & Mercury steel wheels, which were widened and mounted with whitewall tires in typical '50s style. Both cars also had plenty of chrome and nice paint jobs, so they were show winners. One other thing that both cars had was the steering column nearly straight down through the floor.

Tommy Ivo's T-bucket turned up in the pages of *Hot Rod* magazine too (August 1957 and January 1960,) and in many other automotive magazines. Ivo won many trophies with his car, and not just in the shows, but at the drag strip. He drove it to the track, took the high windshield off, bolted a roll cage to the frame, added a set of slicks in the rear, and put on his helmet. His T-bucket became a terror at the race tracks around California, and the powerful Buick motor gave him 11-second runs at more than 125 miles per hour, which must have been a shock to his opponents. Ivo ran the car in the "street roadster" class and went on to win the California Street Roadster Championship with his hot rod. He tried many different carburetor setups, and in the pictures you can see anything from six Strombergs, to dual four-barrels and an injection setup.

Both cars later became even more famous through TV series and movies. Grabowski's T got well known as the "Kookie-car" in the series *77 Sunset Strip* and got its name from the driver, Edd "Kookie" Burns. This way, the car and the style were presented to all the youngsters around the country, who soon wanted to build one of their own. Tommy Ivo was already an actor in a TV series as a kid, long before he built his roadster. After racing the car for a few years, he also drove it on the streets of Southern California. In the late '50s he sold the car to Bill Rolland, who modified it a little bit and repainted it metallic dark blue. Pretty soon he "took it to Hollywood" and got involved in movies. Several "youth movies" were made in the late '50s and early '60s, and the Ivo-T had a part in

The Ivo T had many looks in the movies, and appeared with a top. The wheels he bolted on the car came from a '50 Mercury, and so did the hubcaps. The rear wheels were widened to fit the whitewall slicks, and the front rims were reversed to look deeper. The famous Von Dutch pinstriped the Ivo T, and that was the last car he did. He died some years later.

many of them. Some of the more famous movies were *Dragstrip Girl* (1957) and *Choppers*, in which both Tommy Ivo and the T-bucket had big roles.

Ivo continued to make movies and had parts in more than 100 of them through the years, plus parts in a few TV series. That gave him the nickname "TV-Tommy" Ivo. But he was not just an actor; his passion for drag racing got so strong that he started to run dragsters of all kinds. He drove one-motor, two- and four-motor monsters before he switched to jet cars, top fuelers, and funny cars.

Today, the Ivo hot rod belongs to Jack Rosen, who got it from his dad. Through the '60s and '70s his dad had the car rebuilt into a show-rod by

George Barris. But in the late '80s Jack decided to have Ron Jones restore it to a perfect original shape. The chassis was in sad shape, and a new frame had to be built for the car during the restoration process. All other components were intact, so getting it back to its original shape was possible. When he showed the car after the restoration,

The interior was done in a traditional white Naugahyde tuck and roll style, and Ivo built the dash from tubing and sheet metal. A full set of Stewart Warner gauges is set deep in the dash. The near-vertical steering came from a '41 Ford and was shortened before they mounted it to the frame with a homemade bracket. The pedal assembly and master cylinder also came from the '41 Ford, but Ivo had to modify the pedals to better fit the T.

The front end setup was a copy of the one Grabowski did on his car, with a '37 Ford tube axle, tie-rods for the four-link, and the spring behind the axle with backwards spring perches. The spindles and brakes came from the '41 Ford that Ivo bought and took apart to get all the parts he needed for his project.

Rosen had a purchase offer for about $100,000, but he said "no thanks."

The "Kookie Car" was another story. Owner Jim Skonzakis has it locked up in his garage in Dayton, Ohio, but it bears little resemblance to the original "Kookie Car." In the 1960s it was also rebuilt to be a "show-rod," with twin-blowers and other modifications. Nobody knows if that car will ever be restored to its original look. The car we see here in the pictures is the replica that Franco Constanza built to recreate the great old car. He collected parts and magazine articles for nearly 15 years before he could build the car, but it gave us a true look of what the real "Kookie Car" looked like in its TV series heyday. Today there is another "Kookie-Car" replica, built by Grant Pendergraft in Portland, Oregon, that was shown at the 50th Oakland show.

Many more replicas of these two great hot rods might be built in the future, even if some of the parts are getting harder to get hold of today. These two cars started the Fad-T era, and also inspired people to start the production of the many kit-car Ts that hit the market later. Those kit-car Ts are still available, and still represent many young hot rodders' first attempts to build a hot rod.

The good-looking Ivo-T is still giving hot rodders plenty of great ideas, so many were happy to see the famous old hot rod being restored by Ron Jones. The engine is still the same bored 402-inch Buick with 10:1 Jahns pistons, Winfield cam, and Hilborn injection that took Ivo on many quick trips down the drag strips around California.

FENDERLESS MODEL T & A FORDS

After World War II, from the mid-1940s until the early '50s, lots of hot rods were built in California. Many called them "the roaring roadsters" because they raced some of them on dirt tracks, first on the West Coast, but very soon all over the nation. They created a special class at sprint car races for "hot rod roadsters," and it became very popular with the people in the grandstands. They also drove some of these roadsters on the street, and now and then out to the desert, to do some weekend high-speed racing at dried-out lake beds like El Mirage and Muroc. They stripped the cars of the headlights and windshields, and some owners had tonneau covers to give their cars a little extra streamlining. Some best street-roadsters were running between 125 and 150 miles per hour. In the late '40s they also found the perfect dry lake bed for racing, the Salt Flats in Utah, also called Bonneville. In those days, hot rodders built their cars to be used for all kinds of racing—just a basic little roadster with

Ed "Isky" Iskenderian started to build his '24 T-roadster before World War II in 1939, but it wasn't until after the war that he raced it at El Mirage. The frame Ed used was a '27 Essex that was modified, and the rear end came from a '32 Ford. The unusual thing with the rear end is that the leaf-spring is in the front of the axle. The '32 Ford front axle was mounted with a '37 Ford wishbone, with the leaf-spring in front of the axle, which made the chassis a little lower. Ed made his own grill shell by welding two '33 Pontiac shells together, and the wheels are 16-inch Kelsey-Hays that Ed bought brand new for two bucks each in 1939.

Isky built a special engine for his '24 T-roadster, using a '32 Ford flathead that he bought for $60. Initially, he swapped the stock cam for a Winfield cam, but later he used one of his own cams instead. Maxi-heads, with overhead-style exhaust valves and rockers under the valve cover, plus a Thickstun manifold with three '97 Stromberg carburetors, gave him plenty of extra horsepower.

tuned motor, and no chrome. There was not much speed equipment available, but soon the demand for it created a market. Some racers started to make their own speed equipment, leading to the rise of such companies as Isky Cams, Edelbrock, Offenhauser, and Schiefer Flywheels, to name a few.

Soon there was so much going on with all the different kinds of hot rod races and all the new equipment for hot rods that "Pete" Petersen and some of his friends saw a market for a speed magazine.

In 1948 Petersen started *Hot Rod* magazine, and the first issue was sold from the bed of his pickup at race meets and shows. The magazine spread the message across the nation, and some years later to Europe, Australia, and even South Africa. The magazine showed people how to build a safe hot rod and featured the best of them.

Before that, in the early days, most of the young guys building their cars were looking for a light little roadster, because with less weight it was easier to make it go faster. All the Model-T and -A Fords up to 1931 had four-cylinder engines, and many builders of early hot rods used them, tuned-up for more performance. It didn't take long before they found out that those bodies would fit on top of a 1932 Ford chassis, which came with the first V-8. Tuning that flathead V-8 was easier, so most hot rodders wanted that combination. T- and A-bodies were easy to find in local junkyards or parked in a field. When it came to the 1932 chassis, all the models that year had the same chassis, but some had a four-cylinder engine, so most hot rodders were looking for a chassis with the V-8.

With a Model-A or late T-body on top of a '32 chassis, the hot rodder had a fenderless "highboy." The A-body has a flat "bottom" and the '32 frame a bit of a "belly," so they came up with a

This roadster was driven by "Isky" Iskenderian on the street and at El Mirage, with a best speed of 120 miles per hour on May 8, 1942. Later, Isky became famous for his cam grinding company in Gardena, California, called Iskenderian Cams, or Isky Cams.

piece of wood to fill the gap. It didn't take long before somebody had another good idea: to modify the '32 frame by using a Model-A front cross-member. That cross-member is deeper, so that it dropped the frame more than an inch closer to the ground. Another common modification to drop the front end was to turn the front spring main leaf over, to get the spring closer to the front axle. That dropped the front end another inch. This was before the dropped front axles were introduced to the market and became essential on all hot rods.

The rods of the '40s and early '50s were mostly painted black, but many of them never passed the primer coat stage, or were painted in the backyard. Performance and tune-up equipment was much more of a priority for street racing or weekend hot rod races, so many hot rodders didn't want to spend money on a new paint job. Instead, they bought high-compression aluminum

heads, multi-carb manifolds, and camshafts. Some even used overhead valve conversions, like Ardun heads, and blowers to get extra horsepower. But after the car shows started in 1949–50, some hot rodders went "chrome city" with their roadsters, and got the motors all dressed up. The shows in L.A. and the big "Grand National Roadster Show" in 1950 in Oakland changed much of the hot rod scene, from race cars to dressed-up hot rods.

One hot rodder who became famous was Ed "Isky" Iskenderian, who built his Model-T in 1939. He constructed his black T-roadster on an Essex frame that he bought from his friend, John Athens, for 15 bucks. For power he used a '32

Next Page
A new bracket was made for the '37 Ford steering box, which was mounted on the side, to get the Pitman arm on the outside of the frame. Specialty Cars made a new Pitman arm, to get the arm in the neutral position.

This classic track roadster had to be powered by a flathead V-8, and Tomas found a '52 Mercury 255 engine that was rebuilt and tuned-up a bit with Edelbrock heads. The manifold, from the same company, has two '97 Stromberg carbs, and the ignition system was improved with a Mallory distributor.

Ford flathead motor, which Isky modified with a Winfield cam and a set of Maxi heads. Like many other hot rodders, Iskenderian drove his roadster to El Mirage and raced it. Isky still has his old roadster, but now it is a museum piece at the NHRA museum in Pomona, California. At the time I took the pictures, Isky had the car at Isky Cams in Gardena, California. It had been parked there for years, and Isky said, "let's see if it runs." It started right away when he pushed the starter button.

Another roadster that has meant a lot to hot rodders for decades is Bill Niekamps' '29 Model-A that was built in the late '40s. He built his roadster for desert racing, but it was also street-driven. The front end of Niekamp's roadster has a hand-formed aluminum, streamlined track roadster

Tomas had Josten Solgaard paint the body racing green, then he did the neat leather interior himself. Tomas is a leather-craft designer by trade, so he had no problem picking the brown antique leather for the car and stitching it too. The dash has a pair of '32 Ford gauges in a stock Model A insert, and the steering column, including the steering wheel, is also out of the Model A.

It is easy to see how much Tomas Z-ed the frame behind the body, to get the chassis closer to the ground. A Model T rear spring was mounted on top of the '40 Ford rear end, and the cut wishbone was moved in on the rear end to clear the frame. Check out the neat handmade brackets for the taillights and exhaust system.

nose, and the frame is covered with a "belly pan," all to make it run faster at the lakes. Niekamp had a tuned flathead under the hood, but when today's owner, Jim "Jake" Jacobs, restored the car in the early '70s, that motor was missing. When Jake found the car, it had a Buick nailhead motor that he replaced with an early 265 Corvette engine. After these pictures were taken, the Chevy was replaced with a flathead again, to restore the car to its 1950 configuration, when it won the first "America's Most Beautiful Roadster" trophy at the Oakland Roadster Show. Niekamp worked for Chrysler while the car was built, but he did not even have a welder, so most of the chassis was bolted together. He had good ideas and simple solutions.

Dick Courtney was another L.A. guy who showed other hot rodders how to build timeless roadsters. He didn't build just one classic hot rod; he built three through the years, all black '29 high boys with laid-back Hallock windshields (Duke Hallock was a high school friend of Courtney's). Courtney built the first car in 1946, with a flathead under the hood. Number two was built in the '70s

and number three in the '80s, and both of them have small-block Chevys for power. For the later cars, Courtney had to make his own mold from the windshield he had on the first car. The Courtney high boys are traditional, just like the late Bill

continued on page 31

Next Page

Bill Niekamp built this timeless roadster with a '29 body in 1948. He wanted a roadster to run at Bonneville, but also to use as a street roadster. The chassis needed to be a little stronger than a stock Model A frame, so Niekamp modified a '27 Essex frame and Z-ed it in the rear to get the car low and streamlined. Under the hood you will find a tuned flathead and a '39 Ford transmission. The '29 roadster body was channeled over the frame, and Bill made a belly pan to make the car more streamlined for high speeds at Bonneville. The front end was hand-formed out of aluminum, and a hood was made to fit. This beautiful roadster didn't just run fast at Bonneville with a best of 142 miles per hour, but also won America's Most Beautiful Roadster award at the Oakland Roadster Show in 1950.

Like many of the early roadsters, Bill Niekamp's '29 has a '37 Ford tube front axle with a suicide-type front cross-member and a set of homemade hairpins. Ford '40 hydraulic brakes are used on a set of '39 Ford spindles. Bill built the car at home, and strange enough he didn't even have a welder, so most brackets are bolted to the chassis. He worked for Chrysler when he built the car, so he painted it Chrysler Silver Blue.

The rear end in the roadster is a Ford with a Halibrand quick change center section, to make it easy to change gears at Bonneville. With the belly pan under the car, Bill had the exhaust go through the chassis and out in the rear pan. The rear tube bumper was made to cover the body, when it was used on the street. The owner today is Jim "Jake" Jacobs, who bought the car around 1969 and restored it.

George Lundvall lives in Enköping, Sweden, and is a member of the Prinsbo Outlaws, a club that has traditional hot rods only. Lundvall had a dream about building a flathead-powered Model A roadster after he had been reading old hot rod magazines for many years. Lundvall got some help from his friend, Micke Fors, making the replica '32 frame and fitting it with Model A cross-members front and rear, and dropped I-beam front axle with '39 spindles and '40 Ford hydraulic brakes. A stock '32 wishbone holds the front end in place. The rear end is a '40 Ford with a Halibrand quick change center section with 3.78:1 gears, and suspended with a Model A spring.

Bilekipering in Stockholm, Sweden, did the interior in beige leather, and Lundvall used all Ford parts for the dash and steering. The stock Model A dash has a pair of extra Stewart Warner gauges. The steering column and the steering box are from a '37 Ford, but the unusual thing is the column shifter that Lundvall uses to keep the floor space intact.

The engine is a '49 Ford 100-horsepower flathead that was totally rebuilt. A Reed camshaft and the block was ported and relieved to make the motor breathe a little better. A set of Offenhauser heads gave the motor more compression, and a manifold from the same company was bolted on top of it with three '97 Stromberg carburetors. The headers are a set of old Fentons.

The late Dick Courtney built this '29 highboy roadster in 1946, but he didn't stop there. He built a No. 2 car just like it years later. The last version was completed before he passed away, and Joe Scanlin bought the car from the family. The only big difference in the cars is that the first was the only one with flathead power; No. 2 and No. 3 have small-block Chevies.

All three cars have Hallock windshields made by one of Courtney's friends, Duke Hallock, in the La Habra/Fullerton area of L.A. The latest version that Joe drives has somewhat more modern components, like a Vega steering box connected to the steering column with the four-spoke Bell steering wheel on top. The dash has an Auburn replica insert, and in the other two cars there are stock-type '32 inserts.

Continued from page 25

Burnham–built roadster. His baby-blue high boy has a big-block 400-ci Ford motor under the hood. Burnham drove his roadster all over the West Coast for nearly 20 years before he passed away. Bill was one of the true hot rodders who drove his roadster to Bonneville and left the white salt on the car when he drove it to the big GoodGuys event in Pleasanton, California, the next weekend. When he parked that baby-blue roadster at Pleasanton, everybody knew where he had come from. The car is still a well-known "driver" at many Northern California events.

It is not just in the States that really classic hot rods are built. Scandinavia has many true and timeless Model-A rods, too, like George Lundvall's '31 roadster with tuned flathead motor and Halibrand rear end. He dreamed about a highboy roadster since he was a kid, and he made that dream come true. With all the ideas in his head, it took him years just to find all the parts. Nevertheless, his blue high boy set the standard for many

Under the Jack Hageman–made hood of the high boy, you will find a big-block Ford 390 engine bored out to 400 ci, 10.25:1 pistons, Motorcraft cam, and 428 hi-performance heads. It was topped off with an Edelbrock manifold and a 750 Holley carburetor. Behind the engine is a C-6 Ford automatic transmission.

hot rod builders in Sweden. The same can be said about Tomas Törjesen in Norway, with his track-roadster type '29. The car was finished in 1998, even if it looks like it was built in the mid- or late 1940s. It is very similar to the track-roadsters built in the early days of hot rod races, with a tuned flat-head motor, stretched "modified" wheelbase, and the short front-half '29 Ford body. All these rod builders did most of the work on their hot rods, and their cars are classics.

Most hot rodders have seen this roadster as a drawing, because Bill Burnham wrote a column for *Street Rodder* magazine, and his roadster was illustrated in it. Burnham was one of the few hot rodders that had more than 100,000 miles behind the wheel of his rod. He drove the '29 to Bonneville every year, and then straight to Pleasanton for the big GoodGuys event. His roadster always had some white salt still on the car when he rolled into the fairgrounds at Pleasanton. Burnham passed away a few years ago, but until then he drove his roadster to Bonneville every year for the Speed Week racing. This high boy is as classic as they come. Burnham built the car about 20 years ago and based it on a '32 frame that was extended 4 inches and narrowed 2 inches at the firewall. The front end has an old dropped Merritt I-beam axle, '39 Ford spindles, and '40 Ford brakes with Buick drums. A split wishbone keeps the front end in place. The rear end is a 9-inch Ford that was narrowed a few inches before it was installed with a four-link setup and a pair of coil-over shocks.

1932 FORD HOT RODS

The most appreciated older Ford model, in my eyes, is the 1932 Ford Roadster. It is called the "Deuce," and it has always been a valuable model, even if many more open Fords were made in the '20s. The big deal with this roadster was that you could get it with a flathead V-8 under the hood, which made this car very popular with the hot rodders later. Earlier, only the expensive cars had V-8s, but when Chevrolet outsold Ford with their six-cylinder engine, Henry Ford wanted something even better. They told Ford that it was impossible to produce a car with the V-8 and sell it for less than $600, so he wanted to prove them wrong. In 1931, not even Ford had a designer working full time for the factory, so most of the early designs came

Doane Spencer's roadster is one of the most beautiful rods ever built. He started to modify it in 1937 and was not finished until Spencer came back from the war. George DuVall donated a windshield, and Spencer modified the frame at both ends to get the car lower. The lines are the most classic hot rod roadster style you can find. The beautiful old black roadster has had some famous owners through the years. In the '50s, Doane Spencer got interested in Ak Miller's idea of running the Mexican road race. He started to modify the chassis and replaced the motor with a Y-block Ford. They stopped the race before he was finished, so he sold the car in parts to *Rod & Custom* editor Lynn Wineland. In turn, Wineland sold the unfinished car in 1969 to Neal East, who put the flathead back in it. He drove it for many years before he sold it to the collector Bruce Meyer, who had Pete Chapouris and crew restore it.

The interior of the now-restored roadster owned by Bruce Meyer was upholstered in saddle-tan leather over a 1933 Cadillac seat by Tom Sewell. Spencer had the seat installed to sit a little better than in the stock '32 roadster. When he built the car, Spencer was influenced by hot rod and sprint car racers of that period, and he used a Gordon Scroeder steering box of that type, with the pitman arm on the side of the body.

The flathead '46–48 Mercury was rebuilt by Tom Sparks, and it is the same motor as the later owner, Neal East, used in the car. It is bored out .030 with Jahns pistons, Winfield cam, Johnson lifters, and Lincoln valve springs. Heads and manifold were made by Offenhauser, and there are two Holley carburetors.

from Briggs & Murray. That year Ford brought in Eugene Gregorie as a full time designer, but it is unclear who came up with the final design for the 1932 roadster. It didn't take them long to produce the new car.

On March 29, 1932, Ford showed off his new series of cars in newspaper ads all over the country, and two days later the cars were at the dealers. More than 5 million people came to the showrooms to see the new V-8 Fords, and about 200,000 of them signed on to buy one. Out of the 360,000 cars eventually sold, only about 15,000 were roadsters,

The windshield was donated in 1937 by George DuVall, when a friend of Spencer's owned the car. Later in the late '40s, when Spencer and his wife drove the car all over the country, a set of windshield wipers was installed, and part of a '34 Ford roof was used as a hard top on the car.

and another 13,000 were Phaetons and convertibles, but they became a very important part of the hot rod history. The new engine had a total size of 221 cubic inches and produced 65 horsepower. The 1932 Ford was also one of the first really mass-produced cars.

By the time World War II was over in 1945, all the homecoming military boys needed something to drive, and there were plenty of Fords for sale. Most of the cars were drivers, but some bought cheaper fixer-uppers at the local scrap yards too.

The '32 roadster was heavier than the earlier T- or A-roadsters, so pretty soon the hot rodders unbolted as many parts as they could, to go weekend racing. As with the earlier roadsters, many hot rodders chose to drive their cars fenderless. They also wanted to tuneup the flathead engines, and at the end of the '40s there were plenty of parts for them on the market. The first step was to swap the

old '32 engine for a later '40 8BA flathead motor that was much better for tuning. With the lakes racing and dirt track racing came the quick change rear end center section that made it possible to
continued on page 40

Next Page
Tom McMullen's black '32 roadster with flames became a symbol for *Street Rodder* magazine, which McMullen founded in the 1970s. He bought the roadster in 1955, but it was not until the early '60s that he painted it black and had Ed "Big Daddy" Roth mask-out the flames. McMullen drove it home and sprayed the flames, then returned to Roth to have it pinstriped and the flames outlined. A photo of that version was published on the cover of *Hot Rod* magazine in 1963. McMullen later sold that roadster but built other '32s with the same look but different motor combinations. This is the last version.

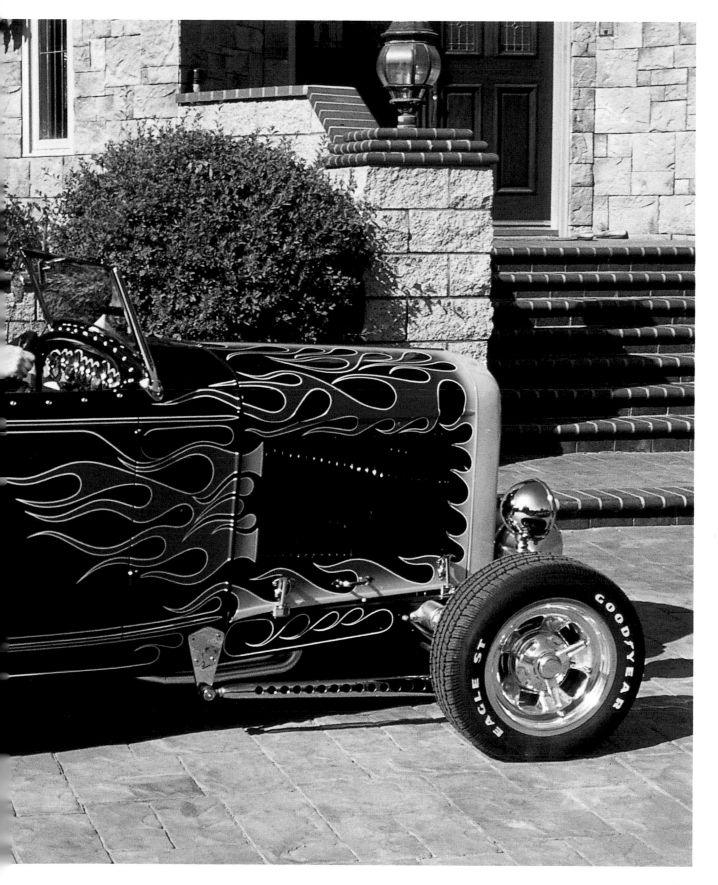

McMullen's last roadster had a B&M blown LT1 small-block Chevy, with TRW pistons, B&M cam, ported heads, and a B&M Megablower on top with two Edelbrock 600 cfm carburetors. The motor was run on B&M's dyno before it was dropped into the roadster, and the results were a stunning 550 horsepower at 7,000 rpms.

Continued from page 25

change gears in the pits. A few of those were introduced on the market, but Halibrand became the best known, and still is today.

There were many styles of '32 roadsters built even in the early days, but a car like Doane Spencer's roadster is a real classic. He streamlined his '32 with a DuVall windshield, and by stripping off the fenders. To get the car lower, Spencer Z-ed the frame both front and rear. That roadster is what hot rodders still use today as a template for the perfect roadster. After being restored by So-Cal Speed Shop, it is in great hands, with collector Bruce Meyer as the owner. With new magazine

One of the most famous pictures of McMullen and his roadster happened by mistake in the early days. McMullen was driving down the road in Buena Park with his then race and street roadster when he released the chute by mistake and a cop on a bike was right behind him. The situation was recreated in front of a photographer the next day for the magazine. This picture is a second reconstruction of the scene with the latest roadster. *Street Rodder* magazine.

The interior of McMullen's roadster was stitched by Darryll "Whitney" Morgan, who did the first roadster in the same black and white tuck and roll more than 20 years earlier. The '32 dash was filled with Stewart Warner gauges, plus plenty of pinstriping. The shifter on the floor is for the five-speed Doug Nash transmission.

features on the restored Spencer roadster, the younger generation hot rodders get their eyes on the classic, too. Meyer wants people to see his classic hot rods, and not have them hidden in a private garage somewhere, so he is showing the roadster and some of his other cars at the Petersen Automotive Museum in Los Angeles.

The first guy to publish my pictures in the United States was Tom McMullen, when he started his *Street Chopper* magazine and later *Street Rodder*. McMullen has had many roadsters through the years, but the most important one was his black and flamed race-style '32. He bought the first of his roadsters in 1958; it had a 283 Chevy motor. McMullen changed the look a couple of times; one of them was with a metalflake paint job, in green. He was not pleased with it, and painted it black later. He was into performance, and replaced the six carburetors on the now-stroked 283 with a 4-71 blower. After McMullen stripped the body and repainted it black, he drove it over to Ed "Big Daddy" Roth and had him lay out some wild flames

on it. McMullen drove the car back home and painted the flames himself. The roadster was one of the fastest "street roadsters" on the West Coast, and McMullen ran it both at the drags and at El Mirage.

In 1963, McMullen and his flamed roadster were on the April cover of *Hot Rod* magazine. One of the most famous shots of the car showed McMullen coming down the street with his chute open and a cop on a bike right behind him. Later, after McMullen sold the car, he wanted to build a modern version of his old roadster, so he built a "new" '32 with a Moser overhead cam Chevy motor in it. Still, it had the same look with flames and all. That car was not a big success, because McMullen had problems getting the motor to run right. Through the years his flamed roadster became a symbol for his *Street Rodder* magazine, and in 1991 he decided to build a new replica of the original roadster. There were a few variations between the new and the original cars, but the look was as close as you could get. It was based on a new replica

With the body channeled over the frame, there was not much floor space for a real seat, so Kassa used two small bucket seats that they upholstered in white vinyl. The 4-inch chopped top also made it necessary for him to sit flat on the floor. As did so many other hot rodders, Andy Kassa used a '39 Ford transmission, with Lincoln Zephyr gears, behind the flathead motor.

frame, had a blown B&M-built small-block Chevy with a five-speed transmission and a replica fiberglass Wescott body. Sadly, McMullen and his wife died in an airplane crash a few years later, but his classic flamed roadster lives on. The magazine has even built another clone, to be a "driver." It has appeared all over the country in events like the Street Rod Nationals.

Not all classic hot rods were built on the West Coast either. Andy Kassa in New Jersey bought his '32 coupe in 1948 and began to modify it. After he chopped and channeled the body, he Z-ed the

Andy Kassa bought his '32 Ford Coupe in 1948, but he kept on changing it until 1964. Kassa lives in New Jersey, and he toured many of the big shows in the '50s and '60s with his chopped and channeled three-window. He did most of the work himself, including Z-ing the frame in front of the rear cross-member and dropping the body 5 inches over the chromed frame. Many remember this coupe because of the "chromed" 268-ci '48 Mercury flathead motor with all the air cleaners. On one of his show tours to the West Coast, Kassa had George Barris make the nose piece in aluminum. The car was then called "The Cyclops," with the single headlight on the left side of the grill. Kassa is more than 80 years old today, and at the time this book was published was in the hospital, so the guys in the local street rod club got together and restored the car. They grew up seeing the car as the best street rod in Clifton, New Jersey, and it is a lot more than that today.

"VonFranco" Constanza is one of the best-known pinstripers in California. He bought and modified this five-window coupe in the early 1990s. When Constanza found the coupe for sale, it was full-fendered with a Chevy Corvair front end and a mid-'60s Chevy rear end. Under the hood it had a tuned flathead and a '39 Ford transmission The old flathead soon created some problems, so he replaced it with a small-block Chevy and a four-speed Muncie transmission.. A guy in San Jose already chopped the coupe in 1951, but Constanza replaced the front end with a traditional dropped and drilled I-beam and a split wishbone. The rear end is now a 9-inch Ford mounted with a pair of long ladder bars.

frame to get the car closer to the ground. Many remember this car from the shows, thanks to the fully chromed flathead motor with four carburetors. Kassa changed the look of the coupe, and during a show tour to the West Coast in the early '60s, he had George Barris make a one-off grill shell. It was used with a single square headlight on the driver's side of the Barris grill. Kassa toured all the big shows from the 50s until 1964, when he parked it in

his gas station garage in Passaic, New Jersey. The car had many names during the time he toured the shows around the country, but most people might remember the last one—"the Cyclops"—with a reference to the single headlight. The car was sitting in his garage until Ron Meola talked to some of his pals in the Meadowlands Street Rod Association. Many of them had seen the car when they were kids, and remembered when Andy used to roll the

It didn't take long before Constanza brought out his pinstriping brushes and totally changed the appearance of the coupe. First he painted the hood and grill shell with white scallops and outlined them in red to match the red steel wheels. The front body panels got "aces and eights" with a pin-up girl painted on each side, before Constanza pinstriped the rear of the body and the dash.

car out of his garage. They talked Andy into letting them restore it as a club project, and they got started in the early '90s. Andy chipped in some money for chrome and paint, and the boys did the work. He came around now and then to check out the project. Then, in 1997, the car was running again, and Andy was very happy with it. The classic was saved. Andy is now 82 years old and has a health problem, but the boys in the club give him a helping hand with what they can.

Franco Constanza, or "VonFranco," as he calls himself is a pinstriper and artist, and just loves old-time hot rods and customs. After he built a "Kookie Car" replica, and sold it, he bought a '32 five-window coupe. He found it for sale in Northern California,

The interior is old-style and might have been done as early as the '60s. The black Naugahyde interior was combined with a stock dash full of old-style Stewart Warner gauges and a fuel-injection hand pump, to the right on the dash. The old banjo wheel and the chromed column drop are original parts from the time in the early '50s when the coupe was chopped.

The front end is a Magnum dropped I-beam axle with a Hollywood spring, and a set of Vinthers-made stainless steel "hairpins" hold it in place. Classic polished Halibrand wheels do a lot to a fenderless hot rod, and the 4.5x15 front wheels were shoed with 145-size Klebers, and the rears are 12x16 inches with 7.50 Firestone dirt track tires.

The roadster has louvers punched everywhere, and the headlight buckets are one place that Mark wanted to have "vented." The top of the hood, the trunk, and the back of the '40 Ford rearview mirror are some of the other places.

Even if Mark Westerick was only 26 years old when he built his roadster, it is screaming "hot rod" with plenty of classic tricks. When Westerick came to California, he already knew who to look up to get some help to build his dream roadster. On his list was Pete "P-Wood" Eastwood, Don Small, and Bill Winthers, so it was natural for Westerick to locate to Temple City, California, where all of them were living. Bill Vinthers built the chassis with a pair of new '32 replica frame rails. Westerick's beautiful roadster has a Westcott fiberglass body on top of the Bill Vinthers–built chassis. The body was modified for the DuVall windshield, and Bill "Birdman" Stewart made the new skin for the trunk and Eric Vaughn did all the louvers. Bob's Paint & Body in Pasadena sprayed the body panels in orange before A&P AutoUpholstery in Monrovia did the black leather interior. The dash has a set of Moon gauges and the steering wheel is an old Ansen product. Under the hood, Mark has a potent LT1 small-block 355 Chevy.

The rod scene has been international for the last 30–35 years, and there are many traditional hot rod builders in Europe. Tommy Classon in Eskilstuna, Sweden, is one of them. He bought this steel roadster in 1992, from an ad in a Phoenix paper, for $12,000. Since then it has been totally restored and rebuilt as an early '50s hot rod. It took Classon a little over five years to build the roadster, and he used only authentic, early hot rod parts to finish his '32. The rear end has a Halibrand quick change center section, and the steel wheels have old-style Firestone tires in 5.50 and 7.00x16 size. The bodywork was done by Ulf Siljemar, and the paint was sprayed by a local paint shop in Eskilstuna. The most impressive part of the finish work was done by Richard Baskin in Fresno, California, who finished the red leather interior during the last 36 hours before the Oakland Roadster Show.

and a guy in San Jose had already chopped the top in 1951. The suspension was not what Franco wanted, so he swapped the Corvair front end for a traditional drilled I-beam axle and a split wishbone. They also replaced the rear end with a later 9-inch Ford, with long ladder bars. He drove the car with the flathead for a while, but it created some problems for him, so he replaced the engine with a small-block Chevy and a four-speed transmission. He also gave it the early rod look by ripping the fenders off and putting some pinstriping and whitewall tires on it.

Another '32 that impressed me was Mark Westerick's orange roadster. Westerick was just 26 years old when he built his roadster. He came to California from Longview, Washington, to work, and he took the opportunity to get the right people involved in his project. If you live in Temple City, California, it is

a "must" to know guys like Pete "P-Wood" Eastwood, Don Small, and Bill Winthers. Winthers built the replica chassis and made a set of "hairpins" to hold the dropped front I-beam axle in place. Westerick has a potent LT1 small-block Chevy under the hood that gives him all the power he wants. The body is dressed up with Eric Vaughn louvers in the trunk lid, hood, headlights and even the back of the '40 Ford rearview mirror. The DuVall windshield and polished Halibrand wheels add to the traditional look. The orange paint job and the black leather interior give the car a perfect finish.

One roadster that has more traveling time than most '32s is Tommy Classon's black show-winner from Eskilstuna, Sweden. As did so many other hot rodders, Tommy had a longtime dream of building a real steel old-time roadster with a flathead. He found the car for sale in Phoenix, Arizona, paid

Only the best was good enough for Classon, and flathead specialist Lennart Djurberg took care of the 1946 59AB motor. The block was bored out for a set of new Jahns pistons, and a 4-inch stroke Mercury crankshaft gave the motor a total size of 284 ci. An Isky 400 Jr. cam plus a set of polished Navarro heads gave Classon some extra horsepower, in combination with a Tattersfield manifold with two Stromberg 97s.

$12,000 for it, and had it shipped back to Sweden. Before Classon bought it, it had been in Australia for years and was sold back to the United States in the early '80s. It was a big project to build the perfect classic roadster, but he had some help from the best in his home country, and he did a lot of work himself. The '46 flathead motor now has all the goodies and is bored and stroked to 286 cubic inches. Everything was restored and built in Sweden except the interior, which was done by his friend, Richard Baskin, in Fresno, California. That was right before Classon took the car to the '98 Oakland Roadster Show and won the Bruce Meyer Award for best nostalgia car. Do I need to say that Classon went home with a smile on his face?

The front end is a drilled I-beam axle with a spring and a drilled and chromed wishbone to hold it in place. The brakes are '40 Ford hydraulics, and the spindles came from a '39 Ford. Classon did much detail work on his roadster, and it all paid off when he shipped the car over the ocean for the Oakland Roadster Show in 1998, where he won the Bruce Meyer Award for the best nostalgia hot rod.

4

1934 FORD HOT RODS

When it comes to '33–34 Ford hot rods, there are a few that stick in your mind, like the ZZ Top coupe, the California Kid, the Super Bell Coupe, or the Pierson Brothers Bonneville Coupe—all of which are classics and famous hot rods. Some people say that coupes are for chickens, but not all of us agree with that. Most well-known '33–34 Fords are coupes, even if many show winners of the Boyd era have been road-sters. The 1933 Ford was very different compared to the 1932 model, with its more streamlined grill shell, fenders, and hood. In 1933, most of the cars had the V-8 engine, and just a few had the smaller four-cylinder. Henry Ford himself was not very happy with the drastic changes between 1932 and 1933. The Great Depression was going on, and

Most of the classic hot rod '33–34 Fords are coupes, but this roadster is a real classic, even if it was built just a few years ago. Öysten Stavdal from Trondheim, Norway, used to build custom VWs, but when he got interested in early hot rods he started to collect parts for a '34 roadster. The chassis was based on a stocker, with updated brakes to later '40–46 hydraulics. No wonder Öysten won a few "best nostalgia rod" awards with his new-old '34 Ford roadster. From the aluminum Buick brake drums in the front, to the E&J bullet-shaped headlights and DuVall windshield on the replica body, it has plenty of class. Larsen's in Öysten's hometown, Trondheim, painted the roadster in British racing green.

It was engine builder Bobby Meeks who talked his friends, brothers Bob and Dick Pierson, into building a streamlined '33–34 Coupe for Bonneville. While Meeks started building a killer flathead motor, the brothers modified a '33 Ford three-window coupe. The rules said 7-inch windshield minimum, but didn't say anything about angle, so they leaned it more than a little bit. The top was chopped 9 inches. The owner today is collector Bruce Meyer in Beverly Hills, who spent a bundle of money to have the car restored to perfect shape. Involved in the project were guys like Pete Chapouris, Jake Jacobs, Bobby Meeks, and Steve Davis, just to name a few. This car was a real winner with 36 wins out of 39. Bob Pierson also ran a best of 153 miles per hour, which was a class record.

Bobby Meeks was working for Edelbrock, so after the 297-ci was built, Meeks ran it on the dyno. The result was outstanding, with more than one horsepower per ci, and in 1949 that was the most powerful carbureted flathead ever. It is based on a '46 Ford block with a Winfield cam, Edelbrock high-compression heads, and manifold with a pair of Stromberg 48s.

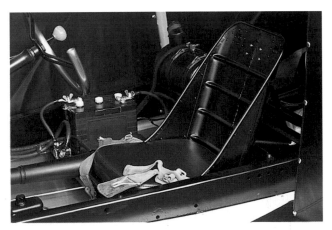

The interior of the Pierson Coupe is all race, and very spartan. They cut out the floor of the body and a new aluminum one was fitted under the frame, so the transmission and torque-tube drive shaft were right beside the driver. It is not a good idea to keep the tank and battery next to the driver, but was OK in those days.

Lennart Djurberg, in Stockholm, Sweden, is an expert in building flathead engines, and Öysten shipped his engine to Lennart to be rebuilt and tuned. The block he based the engine on is a '41 239-ci, but with a Mercury crank from Reath Automotive it gave the motor a total size of 268 ci. You can also find a set of Jahns pistons, Isky cam, valve springs, and adjustable Johnson lifters among the goodies in the motor. A pair of Thickstun covers hides the stock heads, and on top of it is a McCullogh blower and a pair of Stromberg carburetors.

the competition was catching up with Ford's sales. The improvements in the new Ford were many, and included a 6-inch-longer wheelbase and smaller 17-inch wheels. The new car was introduced to the market in February 1933. For 1934 very few changes were made. In essence, Henry got his way by keeping the "Model 40," as it was called.

A moment I will never forget happened one afternoon at Bruce Meyers' house in Beverly Hills, when I was taking pictures of the Pierson coupe in his garage. Meyers said, "Let's take it out for a spin!" Said and done, Meyers and his son took turns driving it up and down the street. I took more pictures. Not many people have seen the

Öysten wanted a stock-looking leather interior that would last forever, and he got some help from Knut Holmstedt to stitch up the upholstery in brown leather over a pair of Vauxhall Viva seats. The dash has both stock gauges and aftermarket Stewart Warners. The steering column and steering wheel are from a '39 Ford. There is no stereo. "The song from the tuned flathead is just perfect to listen to," says Öysten.

It is easy to see that Paul Bos, from San Diego, California, had Tom Prufer's "Cop Shop Coupe" on his mind when he built this flamed '34 three-window coupe. It is nearly impossible to recreate how Prufer's coupe chassis was built, but Bos used '34 frame rails with a '32 frame front piece from the firewall forward, to make the coupe "sit right." The big whitewall "donuts" on painted steel wheels give the car more of a classic style. Bos used a dropped and drilled I-beam front axle, with a pair of hydraulic Ford brakes updated with a set of polished Buick drums. The body is chopped 3 3/8 inches and channeled 3 inches over the frame, and Bos put many hours into getting the replica body's door gaps perfect before it was painted in a Deltron black. The flames were painted by Bob McCoy, and Lyle Fisk did the pinstriping.

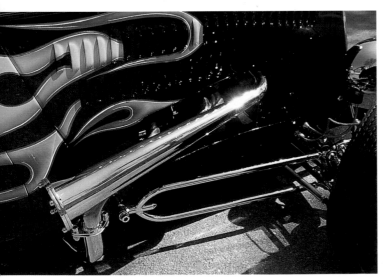

Headers in old "Lake style" fit this type of hot rod very well, and they were made by So Cal Speed Engineering in Costa Mesa, California. The hairpins that hold the dropped I-beam front axle in place were made by T.C.I. Bos made the special three-piece hood and had it punched full of louvers before he took the car to be painted.

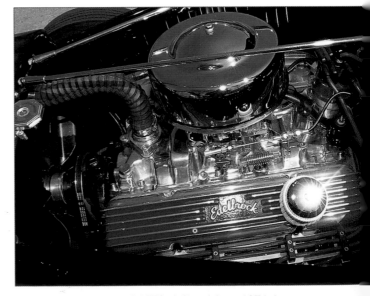

The engine is a mild 350-ci Chevy from 1976 that was rebuilt. When it was put back together, plenty of goodies were used, like a Schneider cam, 2.02-inch heads, and a polished Edelbrock Performer manifold with a 650 Carter carburetor. To keep the engine running smooth, Bos picked a Mallory Unilite distributor.

One of the '34 coupes that hot rodders will not forget is Jim Ewing's Super Bell Coupe. This three-window '34 steel coupe is very radical, and he drove it all over the country to participate in many street rod events. The chopped body was deeply channeled over the frame to give the car a very low roofline, but it is the slim Bonneville-style aluminum nose that gives the coupe its real profile. The Super Bell Coupe has had many different types of wheels, from the original steel wheels with Moon discs to the set of Halibrands pictured here. Ewing sold the car to his friend, Frank Morawski, years ago, before he was killed in an airplane crash. The new owner has kept it the way it was, except for a few details like the interior. The Halibrand quick change rear axle and the big Firestone dirt track tires make this hot rod look mean. *Frank Morawski*

Much of this famous old hot rod's profile comes from the slim Bonneville nose and the big stock headlights, but such a small opening for the radiator posed problems. Ewing had many different motors in the car—everything from a big-block Chevy to a hot small-block and a mild V-6 Buick engine. The Buick engine is still in the car. *Frank Morawski*

Ewing never finished the interior of the car. He finally sold the car to his friend Morawski in the mid-'80s, after having left the car with him for months at a time. The first thing the new owner did was to finish the interior with an upholstered seat and carpeting. With the body channeled that deep and the top chopped, there is not much space left for a seat. *Frank Morawski*

Pierson coupe coming down the road, without lights and plates. It looks even more mean on the street. When Dick and Bob Pierson built the car in 1949, there was a rule in the Southern California Timing Association (SCTA) book about a minimum 7-inch windshield on the coupes. But more chop was better for the streamlining, so they took a chance and chopped it 9 inches, with the windshield posts leaned back as much as possible. That gave them the 7-inch windshield they needed for

His real name is Ove Skoog, but he calls himself "Doc Forest" and is a tattoo artist in Stockholm, Sweden. He won the European Championship a couple of times, and the design of his hot rod is part tattoo and part war plane. With ideas like that the design can be radical. The '34 coupe was built on a Scandinavian Street Rods—made frame that was lengthened 8 inchesThe front end is something that people take a closer look at, because Ove made those shark teeth open and close in the grill. When the motor gets warm, the grill will open and let the air through the radiator. The grill-bullet was made from a '37 headlight bucket, and the bezel made from two VW headlight trim rings. The headlights are hidden behind the "eyes" and are operated by electric motors. Behind the "Flash Fighter" coupe is a restored World War II-vintage P-51 Mustang.

the rules. The Bobby Meeks–built motor was also something very special, with 297 cubic inches and more than that in horsepower. Bob Pierson ran a best of 153 miles per hour with the coupe, and the car was a real winner. They won nearly all the events they ran with the car. At the Muroc meeting in 1997 the Pierson brothers came by the pits and helped out Kjell Gustavsson, who was running his Swedish-built, Pierson-looking, hemi-powered '34 coupe. The brothers also told us that one of them was born in southern Sweden, and the other on the boat to America. The bond with the Swedish team was natural.

It is not often that you run into a neat, classic style '33–34 roadster in Europe. But Öysten Stavdal from Trondheim in northern Norway has turned a lot of heads with his blown flathead machine. I first saw the car at the Swedish Street Rod Nats in Östersund a few years ago. Some of the hot rodders were just standing there staring at the roadster, and I was one of them. It was impossible for Öysten to find a real steel roadster body, so he had to go with a fiberglass replica, against his will. All the other parts could be found. The chassis has the traditional dropped I-beam axle with transverse leaf-springs, and the engine is a '41 flathead

stroked to 268 cubic inches, and it has a McCullogh blower on top with two Strombergs. The racing green exterior and the brown interior make this roadster stand out.

Coupes with flames are always favorites, and Paul Bos' black fenderless coupe is one of them. It has a little bit of Tom Prufer's "Cop Shop Coupe" in the look. Bos cut the '34 frame and used a '32 frame front piece to make the coupe "sit right." "Hairpins," whitewalls, and flames will make any hot rod look great. Bos also added a chopped top and a nice set of headers by So-Cal Speed Engineering in Costa Mesa. It is easy to pick Bos' coupe out of thousands of hot rods at the GoodGuys event at Pomona; it has plenty of tradition and style, and it screams "hot rod."

One event that got many hot rodders thinking about building a '34 coupe was when the late Jim Ewing's "Super Bell Coupe" was presented in *Hot Rod* magazine in 1976. Editorial staff member Gray Baskerville named it "Coupe De Race" and tested it for the magazine. The chopped and channeled '34 with that Bonneville-style streamlined nose was perfect. The 10-inch-lengthened frame in front of the firewall was covered by a Kenny Ellis formed aluminum hood, nose, and frame cover. At the time

Pin-up nose art was painted on fighters and bombers during World War II, and Ove wanted one painted on the trunk of his '34 coupe. Robert Claussnitzer painted the car in white pearl and the flames in candy red, designed by Ove. The pin-up was done by Håkan Wickström.

The choice of engine combination was easy for Ove, and a 350 Chevy was rebuilt before it was put together with a polished Edelbrock Performer manifold, with a 650 Holley. The Speedway aluminum water pump was also polished, and a pair of block-hugger headers gives the motor a little extra horsepower. With all the shine, it still gives 265 horsepower at the rear wheels

Baskerville tested it, Ewing had steel wheels on it with Moon discs. The interior was not finished, but it did not matter at all, because the look was unreal. Ewing drove the coupe all over the country to all of the big street rod events, and he tried different engines in it, from a big, bad big-block Chevy, to a hot small-block and a Buick V-6. He had some over-heating problems with that small front end open-ing, so he ended up using the small Buick V-6 in it. Between the runs to all the events, he left the car many times with his pal, Frank Morawski, in Balti-more, Maryland. Soon, Morawski started to ask Ewing about selling him the car, and that finally happened in the '80s. Morawski finished the interior and put a set of Halibrand wheels on it. He still dri-ves the "Super Bell Coupe."

Maybe it takes an artist and a tattooist to create something like Ove Skoog's "Flash Fighter" coupe. Skoog is a European tattoo champion and has a well-known studio in Stockholm, Sweden. He used the "war bird" style of decorations of the "Flying Tigers," with pin-up girls, checker boards, and even a nose cone to give his coupe some personal style. The front end and the teeth open when he fires up the 350 Chevy engine. The headlights are hidden in the side of the grill and come out when he turns on the lights. Skoog also put many hours of detail work into the interior and the special dash. His collection of neat parts came to good use building the coupe. The paint job gives this car its special profile, and Skoog can be proud of having one of the Swedish hot rods that was published in the U.S. magazines.

Among the very important '34s of hot rod his-tory is Pete Chapouris' "California Kid" coupe. This car got more than well known through the media. It was first published in *Rod & Custom* magazine. After that, it was featured in the movie, *The California Kid* (1974), with Martin Sheen as the driver of the coupe. Chapouris built the coupe right before he and Jake Jacobs got together and formed Pete & Jake's Hot Rod Parts, with their shop in Temple City, California. The Cal-Kid coupe became a symbol for P&J's, and

When Pete Chapouris built his chopped '34 Coupe in 1973, not many hot rodders dared to chop the top of a perfect coupe body. The car that Chapouris bought for $250 was already chopped, but the top was smashed in by kids playing on it. It was painted with flames, and after it was on the cover of *Rod & Custom*, a film producer wanted it for the movie *The California Kid*, starring Martin Sheen. *Pete Chapouris*

The coupe was abused during the making of the movie, so Pete had to repaint the car, fix the fenders and grill shell, etc. Take a look at the movie, and you will see that they used the car as a real hot rod. Under the hood of the coupe there is a 289 Ford motor, trans, quick change rear end, and Halibrand wheels, all from Chapouris' earlier T-bucket. *Pete Chapouris*

has been for all these years. When they sold Pete & Jake's to Jerry Slower in Missouri, the car was included. Slower also built his own version of "The Kid" but based it on a five-window, so it could not be mistaken for the real thing.

Another close friend of Pete and Jake's is Billy Gibbons of the rock group ZZ Top. Gibbons had the late Don Thelan build him a coupe that was going to be the symbol for ZZ Top's next album. That was in 1983. Both the album and the car were named "The Eliminator," and it became the best-known street rod to "non-street rod people." Together with the "Graffiti Coupe," this is the car that got the most exposure through TV. The Eliminator coupe was always on tour somewhere, so Gibbons wanted a clone built. Chuck Lombardo at California Street Rods built that car, and the only difference is that the clone has a replica fiberglass body.

The "California Kid" coupe is still around but now belongs to the owner of Pete & Jake's Hot Rod Parts, Jerry Slower, of Grandview, Missouri. Slower also built a clone of The Kid, but it has a five-window body instead of a three-window.

The ZZ Top "Eliminator" coupe was built by Don Phelan, and this famous rock 'n' roll hot rod has a clone. The coupe was on tour nearly continuously, so Billy Gibbons wanted another coupe just like it to drive. It was built by California Street Rods, and the only difference was that the "clone" has a replica fiberglass body. Small-block Chevy engines power both.

TRADITIONAL HOT ROD BUILDERS

All hot rod lovers have their own heroes to look up to. For me, Tom Prufer is definitely one of them. If you are into traditional hot rods, you will hear his name eventually, particularly if you start talking about nostalgia drag racing. Prufer lived in Los Gatos, California, for many years before he made the move down south to Long Beach, California. The living room at his Long Beach house had sufficiently large glass doors to make it possible for his '60s front-motor dragster to be on display in there. A spare blown 392 hemi was sitting in one corner, too. It is not easy to sum up his active hot rod life, which still goes on.

Prufer was born in Hamburg, Germany. When he was very young, his family immigrated to Canada. They did not stay there long, and Detroit, Michigan, became their new hometown. It was the end of the 1940s and early '50s, and Prufer grew up seeing a lot of homemade hot rods in his neighborhood. "I still remember a chopped '36 Ford Coupe that was parked outside a parts store, close to where we lived," says Prufer. "It took me some time to figure out how they made the roof that low."

Tom Prufer liked Pete Chapouris' "California Kid" coupe so much that he built this full-fendered three-window '34 coupe. All his cars have plenty of louvers, pinstriping, and a "kick-ass motor." This coupe is one of the few full-fendered cars that Prufer has built through the years, but you can still see in the details that this is a Prufer hot rod.

Prufer has had many '29 Ford high boys through the years, and this is a typical traditional Prufer high boy on a P-Wood '32 chassis. Halibrand wheels and "Tommy the Greek" pinstriping also follow the "100 Pruf" recipe. It has a small-block Chevy under the hood.

When Prufer was about 16, he ran away from home and found a job at a farm in Nebraska. He worked there for two years before he moved west and ended up in Tucson, Arizona, where he went straight to the Air Force base to sign up. It was around 1952 that he built his first hot rod, a channeled '32 Ford roadster. "In those days we didn't worry too much about the details: half a firewall, nearly no floor, and I sat on a box with a blanket over it," recalls Prufer with a smile. "There was not much to think of then: Red or gray primer? With or without whitewalls? One or two extra carbs or a cam was much more important, because the only thing that counted was to have the fastest car in the neighborhood. We built our cars for street racing in those days."

Some weekends Prufer and his friends took the long trip to L.A. to see some real drag racing at the Santa Ana Dragstrip. On one of those trips, Prufer brought his grill shell and the tailgate off his '29 roadster pickup, and went to the pinstriper Von Dutch to get them striped by "The Master."

In 1958, Prufer moved to Northern California and found a job at the Lockheed Aircraft factory, and he has worked for the company ever since. He got deeply involved in drag racing, on a hobby basis, and built a few dragsters and altereds. The first car that he entered in the Oakland Roadster Show was a drag race car in 1958, and up to 1964 he only entered race cars. But from 1964 on, it was hot rods again. "Lowered, louvers, and loud pipes was still the way to do it," Prufer continues. "Yeah! A hot rod should have plenty of louvers and be pinstriped." Most of his hot rods during the years were pinstriped by his friend, "Tommy the Greek."

Prufer has won many trophies with his hot rods through the years, but never the "America's Most Beautiful Roadster" trophy at the Oakland Show. In 1972 he entered the show with a black '29 high-boy roadster that won second place. Maybe he should have won, because people booed that decision. He is very popular with the people who keep coming back to the show every year, and has been elected into the Hall of Fame.

The hot rod that became the most famous of Prufer's cars was the "Cop Shop Coupe." "That

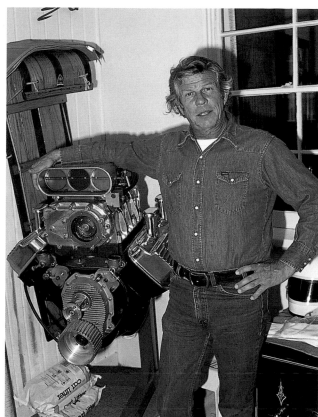

When Prufer lived in Long Beach, he had his nostalgia dragster parked in the living room and the spare blown Chrysler motor on a stand in one corner. Today he lives in Missouri. Although he said years ago that he had built his last hot rod, he has hot rodding in his blood and cannot give it up. He built a new '29 highboy roadster when he got to Missouri!

was the worst car I ever built," admits Prufer. "Pete Eastwood had to build the frame twice before it was right." It was a combination of a '34 back half and a '32-looking front half of the frame. Dave Yuhara and Ron Covell did the bodywork, chopping the top and grill shell and fabricating the complicated hood. "It gave the car the right style that I was looking for," says Prufer. It is still probably the best-looking '34 hot rod Coupe ever built.

The car that has gotten the most ink is this '34 coupe built from a drawing by Dave Bell in *Street Rodder* magazine, and called the Cop Shop Coupe. P-Wood did the chassis twice before Prufer was happy with it, and it is a '34 back half-frame with a '32-type front part. That gave the coupe the perfect rake. The body was chopped and dropped over the frame to make the car very low. *Geoff Carter*

The last car Prufer built in California was this neat three-window '32 coupe with a "kick-ass big-block" under the hood. A quick change rear end, plenty of louvers, and "Tommy the Greek"-type pinstriping make it scream a "100 Pruf" hot rod. What was the first thing Prufer did when the car was finished? He stepped on the loud pedal and did a "donut" at the intersection near his house. "I had to show my neighbors that the car was finished," said the 64-year-old with a smile.

Erik Hansson usually has at least two or three cars in progress at all times for hot rodders all over Scandinavia. Since Brookville began producing the pieces for an all-steel replica '32 Ford roadster body, Hansson has built five new bodies with a combination of parts made by him and Brookville. Three of the first roadsters' bodies can be seen in this picture. *Kjell Gustavsson*

Even before Brookville began to stamp out the pieces for the '32 roadster, Hansson made his own replica parts. When it was possible for him to buy the quarter panels from Brookville, he could build his new bodies. There are more pieces in a '32 roadster body than you might believe. Today he is buying most of the '32 parts from Brookville to save time and money. *Kjell Gustavsson*

The latest roadster Hansson built is this Doane Spencer clone for *Power Magazine*'s editor, Kjell Gustavsson. The only big difference is the big early-hemi engine with injection. For a project like this, it is not easy for Hansson and Kjell Gustavsson to find all the right parts, like the Schroeder steering box out of a sprint car. *Kjell Gustavsson*

Prufer has shown 26 cars at the Oakland Roadster Show through the years, and the last one was a red '32 three-window Coupe with a big-block Chevy under the hood. It was finished just in time for the '93 show, and Prufer vowed that it was going to be his last hot rod and would never be sold. A year later he sold the coupe anyway, then Prufer retired and moved to Sinica, Missouri, with his girlfriend. Talking to him on the phone in 1994, he gave me the news that he was building another '29 Ford high-boy roadster. Hot rodding is too much a part of Prufer's life for him just to give it up, so he will show us how to build real classic hot rods for a long time to come.

There are plenty of traditional hot rod builders outside the United States, too, and one of them is Erik Hansson in Strömstad, Sweden. He has been building hot rods and street rods for the last 20 years. The 1970s was a decade when it was illegal to build street rods in Sweden, but when the government changed the laws in favor of the hobby of

Gustavsson's roadster is taking shape, but Hansson also knows that since he is dealing with magazines, he will have a deadline coming up pretty soon. Hansson is an amazing hot rod builder who recently took a year off to build a new, big building, with a perfect combination of his shop and home in one. The shop size is 800 square yards, and even has a conference room for meetings with customers. *Kjell Gustavsson*

With the first new steel replica body that Hansson completed, even before Brookville presented their roadster body, he figured it would provide plenty of good PR to have a car rolling by the time of the first European Street Rod Nationals (ESRN) in Holland in the summer of 1996. The only problem was time. Hansson drove his "Metal 1" roadster to the ESRA event, after having built the car and the body in just four months. He made all the body pieces except the quarter panels

restoring and building home-built cars, Erik was ready. He started to produce his own '32–34 frame rails and frames a few years before the new laws were passed in 1982.

The market in Scandinavia is not big enough to let Hansson have a large staff, so most of the time it has been a one-man show. He makes everything from frames to turn-key rods, and most of them are '32 Fords. The first car Hansson built for a customer was a replica '32 roadster for *Power Magazine* in 1983, and then a '27 Ford roadster in Bonneville style for *Wheels* magazine. Since then, he has built about 20 complete cars, plus 250 pairs of '32–34 frame rails.

Hansson is also a good metal man and does all the body work on his cars. When companies like Brookville started to produce the panels for a steel '32 roadster body, Hansson bought five sets of quarter panels. With those at home in the shop, he made his own parts for the rest of the bodies. His first steel replica body was finished at the same time that Brookville showed off their first complete body. Hansson finished the body and built himself a roadster in four months. He named it "Metal 1." Only one of the four bodies was sold, and the others were used on roadsters built by Hansson for other customers. The last one of those bodies was used for a new '32 roadster in Doane Spencer style for Kjell Gustavsson of *Power Magazine*. Gustavsson is an early hemi-fan, who also has an injected hemi Pierson Brothers–style '34 coupe that he has run at Muroc and El Mirage. The motor in the roadster is an injected 354-ci Chrysler, and the rear end is a Halibrand Quick Change. The fenderless roadster also has a DuVall-type windshield and a real traditional classic style.

Hansson is a fan of the older classic hot rods, so he prefers to build this kind of car for his customers. Scandinavian hot rodders are very happy to have a craftsperson like Hansson to go to when they need help with their new cars.

P-Wood not only builds traditional hot rods, but restores vintage cars in his spare time. Eastwood's father restored early Buicks when P-Wood was a boy, so he has been around vintage cars all his life. The car in the background is a 1908 Buick, and the other one is a 1933 Miller Indy 500 winner.

Another traditional '32 highboy chassis being built in P-Wood's shop. He cannot even count how many chassis he has made in the last 20 years. Tube cross-members make it easy to fit the exhaust system through the chassis.

Some people call him "P-Wood"—short for Pete Eastwood. This guy is not sitting around waiting for things to come to him. If you never had met him, you might believe that he is much older, because his name has been heard since I can remember. But in 1999, he was not even 45 yet. P-Wood grew up in Pasadena, California, and has been around old cars all his life—his late father was a longtime restorer. P-Wood's first car was a Model T in parts, which he bought when he was 11. At 17, he bought his next car, a Model A. Within a few years he was deeply involved in hot rodding, and started working for the famous Blair's Speed Shop, in Pasadena, California. It was there that he met Pete Chapouris, who sometime later founded Pete & Jakes with Jake Jacobs. P-Wood started his own shop next to Pete & Jake's in Temple City. They became a team and did many projects together throughout the years.

During the P&J days, P-Wood had a '32 three-window coupe with a 327 Chevy that he drove for a decade (1970–80). P-Wood is also a heavy right-foot hot rodder who likes to step on it. His motto is "ride 'em, wreck 'em and never check 'em," but he is not as bad as he sounds. He put more than 100,000 miles on that coupe before he sold it. Right after that, he built a '32 roadster, which he remembers very well, because he finished it on Christmas Eve in 1980. A couple of years later he sold the roadster and started on another high-boy

'32 chassis. That became perhaps his most famous car. Together with his friend Rick Barakat, they created the Eastwood & Barakat Special, with a chopped '32 Tudor body on the high-boy chassis. It was a $4,000 street and race fenderless Sedan that Gray Baskerville of *Hot Rod* magazine called "the world's fastest rusto-rod." Eastwood put some slicks on it and ran it at Orange County Raceway to a best of 11.59. The car was featured in *Hot Rod*'s November 1982 issue, and later it was endorsed by the magazine as one of the "all-time best hot rods," in primer and all. P-Wood says that the idea of the car was to "keep the cost down, so you are not married to it."

Increasingly, P-Wood was building traditional rod chassis for many of the best cars on the West Coast. Then, at night, he was building and restoring his own cars, like vintage Buicks and a Miller race car that won the Indy 500 in 1933. The only problem with restoring odd race cars like the Miller is that there are no parts to be found, and Pete has to make everything. During the past few years Pete worked for Pete Chapouris again at So-Cal Speed Shop, but today he is back home in his own shop building chassis and doing metalwork. Hot rodding and nostalgia racing are also part of his roots, so when they fire up some old Top Fuel or Altereds at Famoso Raceway in Bakersfield, it might be P-Wood in the driver's seat.

Some hot rodders help others to build cars with old Ford parts, which makes the parts live on. Vern

The '32 Coupe that P-Wood drove during the '70s had a 327-inch motor under the hood and was backed up by a TH 400 transmission. He put more than 100,000 miles on the odometer before he sold the coupe in 1980. *Pete Eastwood*

The next car that P-Wood built after he sold the coupe was this red '32 roadster. Here it is parked next to Jake Jacobs' 1950 Oakland Roadster–winning '29 track roadster. The red roadster was used as a typical, traditional roadster in a magazine test, and P-Wood was the test driver. The classic "leaf-spring" P-Wood roadster was nearly as fast on the skid pad as a full independent suspension roadster. *Pete Eastwood*

One of the most famous P-Wood–built hot rods was this fenderless '32 Ford Tudor that Gray Baskerville at *Hot Rod magazine* called "the world's fastest rusto-rod." P-Wood and his friend, Rick Barakat, built the car in a couple of weeks, then drove it to Orange County Raceway, put a pair of slicks on it, and P-Wood ran some fast 11.50 runs with it. *Pete Eastwood*

Pete Eastwood is well known for his heavy right foot and has been a driver for some owners of nostalgia drag race cars. P-Wood restored this "Samurai" dragster with a blown early Chrysler hemi, and drove it at nostalgia meets for a few years. *Pete Eastwood*

No wonder Vern Tardel is smiling, with all the amazing stuff he has in his shop in Santa Rosa. He is "Mr. Traditional," and builds chassis and cars for his friends, most of them flathead-powered. In the shop you can find everything you need to build a classic hot rod, like the '32 three-window coupe he is leaning on. "I build good classic 'drivers,'" says Tardel. "No show stuff."

Tardel is one such hot rodder, and he builds basic classic hot rods in his shop in Santa Rosa, California. It is an amazing place to visit, and if you are into this kind of hot rod, it is heaven. But the problem for him is to find the time to work on his projects, because so many like to contact him for parts and advice. He solved that problem by not having a phone, just a fax machine. The first thing you see when you get there is about 100 old cars in the yard, from early '27 Ts up to '50s trucks and cars. But you also see flathead motors everywhere—even indoors—together with Halibrand Quick Change rear ends and '32 parts. Wherever you look, you'll find hard-to-find parts.

To make it possible to build stock-type '32 Ford frames, Tardel uses a combination of new replica frame-rails and old cross-members. But even the stock '32 K-member can be a problem to find sometimes, so he has started to make his own replica K-members. This way, he can still build the basic "Deuce" frame, inexpensively, too. When I stopped by to visit in 1999, Tardel had some neat cars on which he was working. A T-Phaeton with 289 Ford power, a '32 three-window coupe with a flathead, and a couple of roadsters—a '32 and a '29 with a small-block Chevy. The first thing he said was, "Look around and check out anything you can find." And basically you can find all the good stuff you need for a traditional hot rod. It looks like he could build classic rods for the next 10 years without even calling anyone for parts.

This very low '32 chassis in one corner, with "suicide"-type front end and the frame Z-ed in the rear for the low look. Looks like it will be a "Doane Spencer roadster-type" chassis with a flathead. Note the open modified stock cross-member.

This T-Phaeton had a skinny T-frame, so Tardel replaced it with a much better Model A frame, with stronger cross-members. The engine is a 289 Ford with a C-4 transmission and the rear end is a Maverick 8-inch. The suspension is traditional with split wishbones and transverse leaf-springs.

It is an amazing place Tardel has, and it has taken him 30 years to collect all the parts and cars he has today. Some cars in the picture belong to friends and need some work done on them.

Chapter 6

HOT RODS AT BONNEVILLE, EL MIRAGE, AND MUROC

The development of hot rodding, especially when it comes to performance parts for the engines, would not have become what it is today without the lake-bed racing at El Mirage, Muroc, and Bonneville. The hot rodders in the L.A. area got started in the late 1930s, and

Dean Moon of the Moon Company was driving this chopped '32 Sedan in the late 1950s. The picture was taken at El Mirage, and Moon taped up the grill with a calendar when he ran it on the track. Even in those days they knew about streamlining and the little details that could help. *Greg Sharp*

Gil Ruiz's candy red '29 No. 471 roadster is driven by Bob Beatty to speeds of more than 214 miles per hour, on gas. The injected 302 Chevy engine can also be run on a mix of methanol and nitro, and that would give them plenty more horsepower. The car was built on a Deuce Factory '32 frame with a fiberglass '29 roadster body that was reworked and painted by Sam Foose.

This C/Street Roadster with a big-block Chevy under the hood is owned and driven by Paul Winson. Here it is ready for a run along the long black line at Bonneville, and the driver hopes that the speed on the time card will say 200+ miles per hour. This roadster used to have a tuned flathead Ford motor under the hood, and this owner will rebuild this car with a flathead for Bonneville in 1999.

soon were racing one another on roads close to their towns. The cops were not happy at all with the wild hot rodders and their stripped-down Fords. They got a bad reputation from all the street racing, but soon some of them drove their cars out of town for some weekend racing in the desert instead. One of the favorite places was the dry lake bed at El Mirage. Out there they could test their hot rods all-out for speed. El Mirage is a dry lake about 100 miles from L.A., near Edwards Air Force Base, where the SCTA is still running speed trails six weekends a year.

In the early days, hot rodders sometimes ran more than one car at a time; even four-to-six-cars-wide was not uncommon. When they came out there, they stripped the cars of windshields, headlights, etc., to get a little bit more streamlining. Most hot rodders didn't have any safety equipment at all—no belts, no roll bars—and most of them just wore a T-shirt because of the desert heat. Safety in lakes racing has come a long way since those early days, with full roll bars, fire extinguishers, and full protective fire suits for the drivers.

The only problem with El Mirage is that the lake bed is dry clay, so it will break up and become very

The flathead expert and journalist Frank Oddo teamed up with John Hasford to run this "drop tank" D/Gas lakester with a tuned flathead. They have been running the lakester for many years and have been chasing that class record for as long. Today there are not many "drop tanks" running, but this team is always at Bonneville.

This bright red '29 roadster on '32 frame rails is run in E/Fuel Roadster by Bob Gregg Racing from Santa Ynez, California. It is an example of a neat little 200+ miles per hour roadster that is kept in perfect shape. After a week on the salt, the cars had to be taken apart totally and some parts repainted, because the salt eats up the paint and makes everything rust quickly.

Previous page
Dennis Varni is one of the Northern California hot rodders who put a bunch of money into building a very potent "drop tank" lakester and got a membership in the famous 200 miles per hour club. The lakester has one of the injected all-aluminum, ex-Little John Buttera Indy Cart small-block Chevy motors tucked in the lengthened drop tank.

dusty after running cars for half a day. It is not very long, either, so the course is just 1.33 miles, which means that the real fast cars cannot get up to speed there. They still have plenty of people in the 200 miles per hour club. There are more old stories about hot rodders wrecking their rods going to and from the dry lake than there were crashes running at El Mirage. It was not much of a road that led to El Mirage in those days, and the hot rodders were standing on the gas to get there. Many ran off the road and ended up in ditches, especially after dark, when they had a problem seeing where they were going. While at the dry lake, most of them had sleeping bags and slept under their cars. The place was named El Mirage because when a car, or anything

They line the roadsters up early in the morning, and the lines are filled up all day. At Bonneville there are two courses, one shorter three-mile, out to the left, and the long five-mile course for cars faster than 175 miles per hour. At Speedweek in August, the heat out there on the salt is more than 100 degrees most good days, so the drivers have umbrellas to get some shade during the waiting time in line.

This nice '29 Ford roadster has a small 302-ci Donovan hemi under the hood and is run by John Mackenzie and Robert Waddill. The detail work on the roadster is super nice, with a perfect dark candy red paint job, and the car is run in the D/Gas Roadster class.

Carl Fjastad is one of the sons of Roy Fjastad, who created the Deuce Factory and made the first replica frame rails. Carl started Deuce Frame Co. and has been building '32 Ford chassis for many customers around the country. Bonneville racing is in the blood of the Fjastads, and Carl is running this channeled '32 five-window coupe with an injected small-block under the hood. Best speed has been just under 200 miles per hour.

else, is going across the lake bed, it looks like a "mirage" floating a few feet over the surface.

After World War II, when many hot rodders came back from the war, the SCTA was getting the backing of all the different small clubs. The first elected president was Wally Parks, who a year later left his regular job at GM to work full time for SCTA. They were now running races at El Mirage and elsewhere, but the thing that was at the top of their list was to get a permit to run at the Salt Flats in Utah. The SCTA people soon found out that it was the Chamber of Commerce in Salt Lake City that was in charge of the Salt Flats. The Chamber of Commerce already had formed a Bonneville Speedway Association for people who were trying to run for the Land Speed Record. The salt flats stretch out nearly 90 miles, so there was no problem to lay out a 9-mile-long course out there. The hot rodders could go as fast as they wanted at Bonneville, and the flat, hard salt was like a dream come true for lakes racers.

Soon, Wally Parks, Robert Petersen, and Lee Ryan drove to Salt Lake City to meet with the people there and sort things out. By the time all the paperwork was done and it was time for the first time trials on the salt, it was 1949. The little town of Wendover, right on the border between Nevada and Utah, was filled with hot rodders and their trailers with race cars. Hot rodders could be found at all the motels in town, working on their engines at night, trying to get ready for the next day of racing. About 60 cars took part in that race, so it was a big

Continued on page 89

Next Page

This team used to have Dennis Varni as a partner, but today it is Tom and John Walsh and Tom Cusack, with Justin Walsh in the driver's seat. The roadster is run in B/Blown Street Roadster and is a 200+ miles per hour car. The tank in front of the grill shell gives the car a little bit more streamlining, because a '32 grill becomes like a wall in front of the car at high speeds.

Frank Oddo and his team rebuilt and painted this lakester black with flames. They ran it at Muroc and have been trying for a long time to get in the 200 miles per hour club. This Redi-Strip sponsored "drop tank" lakester has been racing since anyone can remember.

The Pierson Brothers' coupe has been running at Bonneville all these years, but with different drivers, engine combinations, and owners. In the early '90s, collector Bruce Meyer bought the car and had Steve Davis and the Chapouris team restore the old racer to the original shape, with a tuned flathead for power.

The first thing you'll see when you get to the end of the road to Bonneville is this sign that the U.S. Department of Interior has put up. This is to make sure that people know what to do and what not to do on the salt.

Alex Xydias had a race team in 1946 with three cars, sponsored by his So-Cal Speed Shop. This coupe which is now owned and driven by Jim Travis, was part of that team. It was built after the Pierson Brothers' recipe, with the extremely chopped top and laid-back windshield.

Often there is a long waiting time in line at Bonneville, before famous starter Bob Higbee tightens the belts and gives the driver the last few tips about the course. Bonneville is one of the few places on land where you can see that the earth is round, and the cars will disappear behind the horizon.

At the Muroc Reunion you will see more basic hot rods than at any other event, and a very popular combination is the '28–29 Ford roadster high boy on a '32 Ford frame, with a tuned flathead motor. The finish is not that important, but using the right old-style parts is. Wheels are either 16 inch wires or steelies, and the rear end has a quick change center section in most cases.

The new generation of hot rodders and their clubs line up their cars at Muroc. It's like things have started over again in the '50s with the modern generation. They try to mimic the look and lifestyles of that era and know more about the '50s than the old rodders who were part of it.

Barney Navarro has manufactured manifolds and heads for flatheads during the past 50 years. Navarro's old '27 Ford roadster built for lakes racing has been restored during the past few years, and it has a blown flathead with four Stromberg carbs on top, under the bubble on the hood.

Continued from page 83

success and a very important step for hot rodding.

At the first Bonneville race, it was mostly Ford and Mercury flathead engines that dominated. The first type of cars used as race cars were mainly roadsters, because it was easier to strip them of unnecessary parts to get them more streamlined. But pretty soon they created a class for coupes, too, and then came all the classes for stock-bodied cars and even trucks.

Today, nearly 50 years later, you can see all kinds of cars, trucks, and bikes run at Bonneville. The racers keep coming back every year with a new motor or two, to try to set a new record. Some racers have

Some of the competitors travel a long way to be part of the Muroc Reunion, and Kjell Gustavsson came all the way from Sweden with his injected early-hemi—0powered '34 coupe in Pierson style. The team ran a best of 182 miles per hour, and is still looking for that extra fine-tuning to give them that magic 200 miles per hour run.

The Reunion events at Muroc and NHRA's nostalgia drag meet at Famoso in Bakersfield have influenced some of the younger generation to build nostalgic hot rods like this neat '33 Ford Coupe. Black primer is the most common color on all the new generation rods, and it is encouraging to see that many are using the early '50s engines like Cadillac and Oldsmobile Rocket 88.

tried to beat a class record for years and years, and that is a part of the game. Many cars are still the same old cars. They never get old—they just keep coming back. The neat thing about Bonneville is that rules are very traditional, so even cars built today for the hot rod classes look like those of the early days. But they have updated the rules through the years, with better safety requirements for participants and vehicles.

Bonneville Speed Week, like the name says, is a week of speed trails on the salt. Many lakes racers, such as the fast streamliners, run this event exclusively every year. Most race teams come to Bonneville loaded with a couple of engine combinations and all the spares. With a swap for a different size motor, they can run in another class and try to qualify for another record run. People come from all over the world to see and take part in the event, and some of the factories even sponsor racers to run their cars in a near-stock shape to try for a new record.

With Bonneville, El Mirage, Muroc, and the local hot rod racing at the dirt tracks, they created a big market for performance parts in the late '40s, and it was the hot rodders themselves who started

to make the new parts. Guys like Stu Hilborn, Paul Scheifer, Vic Edelbrock, Ed Iskenderian, and Dean Moon were just a few of the rodders who began to manufacture their own products because they could not find the parts they needed on the market.

The first streamliner for lakes racing was built by Bill Burke in 1946, after he found a drop tank of a P-38 fighter plane for sale for $40 in a local surplus scrap yard in L.A. Burke came up with the idea of using the streamlined, two-part aluminum drop tank as a body for a lakes car. He then used '30s Ford axles and a tuned flathead Ford engine for his extreme new streamliner. After he took his invention to El Mirage in 1946, a lot of other racers picked up on his idea. The traditional wing tank streamliners can still be seen at Bonneville, Muroc, and El Mirage, and some of them are running flathead motors too, just like in the old days.

The first race at Muroc took place in the late 1930s, but in 1941, when the United States got involved in the war, the Air Force took over the area and created Edwards Air Force Base. The old Muroc lake bed was then off limits for hot rodders.

New cars are being built today for the hot rod classes at El Mirage/Muroc and Bonneville, thanks to today's repro bodies and frames. This 1932 roadster owned by Norm Kitching from Los Altos, California, has a small-block Chevy under the hood. In addition, this roadster can be street driven if the roll cage is unbolted and the mufflers are bolted back on.

This is one of my favorite cars, Dick Craft's blue T-roadster with a tuned flathead. The car was built in '48, and Craft ran it at El Mirage to a best of 132 miles per hour. In 1950 he had this car at the Oakland Show, too. This nice little roadster is a good example of the street, race and show roadsters of the time. *Greg Sharp*

It took until 1995 before SCTA could talk the Air Force into letting them organize a Muroc Reunion race at the old lake bed. The Air Force used the dry lake bed as it was, and could land fully loaded bombers and, later, 747s without even leaving any tread marks. It is still hard as concrete, and still good for running speed trails. The first reunion was like starting all over again. Wally Parks and other famous old rodders, including some of the old guys that ran in the first few years, came out to see the cars run again at the legendary Muroc.

The first SCTA Bonneville race took place in 1949, and it was a huge success, with 60 cars running during the event. Here are some of the cars lined up for the first time trails. The No. 13 streamlined '27 T to the right is Ak Miller's, and No. 36 in the middle is Fred Carillo's. *Greg Sharp*

El Mirage, 1950. Many of the cars that lined up for a run were street roadsters from the L.A. area. Chrome and whitewall tires were beginning to be used on hot rods at this time. The '29 body on a '32 chassis was a very popular highboy combination, and most owners used a flathead for power. *Greg Sharp*

This early shot is from El Mirage in 1932, and the racers stripped their Model Ts to get a lighter, more streamlined car. The No. 24 car is Frankie Lyons' with a four-port Riley motor, and the No. 6 car the Neal & Halfhill four-port Riley. *Greg Sharp*

A very positive part of the reunion is that the new generation of hot rodders has nearly made the Muroc race into a cult thing. Today you can see more early-style hot rods in primer at that race than anywhere else, thanks to the new generation of hot rodders and their clubs. The Choppers, Shifters, and Lucky Devils are some of the clubs that drive their classic hot rods to the Muroc event, and some of the members bring their girlfriends. They are reliving the '50s today, with hot rods, music, and dress, and they know more about the '50s than most people. They know all about the old cars and how they were built. If anybody is looking for the roots of hot rodding, the best place to start is at El Mirage, Bonneville, or Muroc!

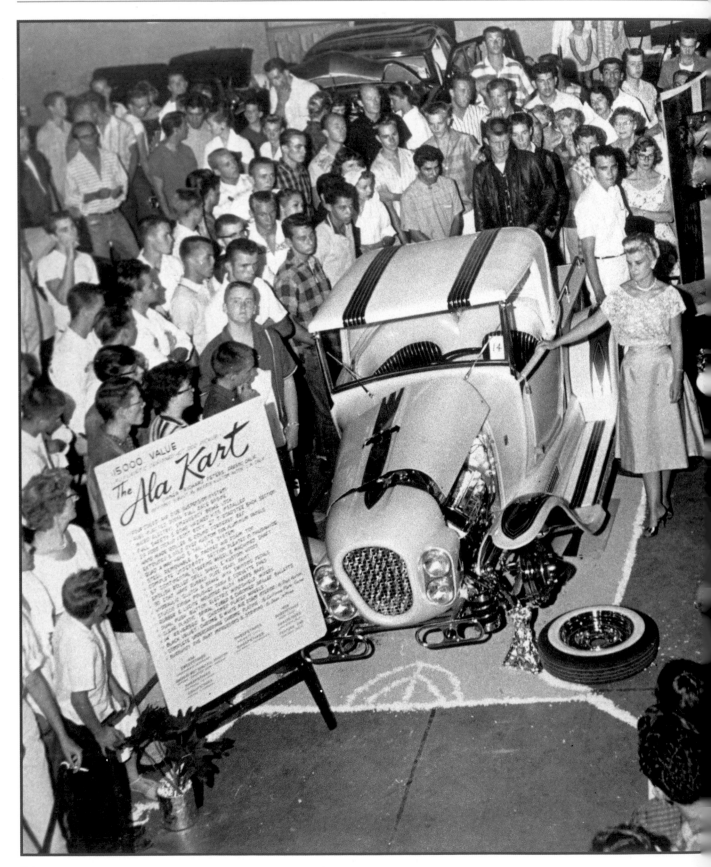

THE OAKLAND ROADSTER SHOW

Al Slonaker produced his first automotive show at the Exposition Building in Oakland in 1949. It was an international car show featuring new automobiles. A local hot rod club from the Bay Area talked Slonaker into letting them exhibit their best hot rods at the show. After looking at the cars, he gave them a corner of the building. There were 10 hot rods on the floor when it was time to open the doors. Before that first show was over, Slonaker found out that those hot rods were very popular, and more people were looking at them than at the new, exotic sports cars. So he changed the plan for the 1950 show and made it a hot rod show instead. The clubs were very happy about it, and the only problem he ran into was that the local newspapers would not print anything that included a term as disreputable as "hot rods," with its connotations of speed-crazy hoodlums. The only way Slonaker could advertise the show was to use other wording, and that's how the name "Roadster Show" came about. Slonaker devised a plan to have a competition for "America's Most Beautiful Roadster." The trophy had to be something

George Barris' "Ala Kart" debuted at the show in 1958 and won the AMBR award, not only that year, but in 1959, too. It was valued at $15,000 at the time. The roadster pickup was a mix of '29 Model A and '27 Model T body parts, and the chassis was very special with coil-springs and airbags in all four corners. *Barris Archives*

that people would never forget, so a 9-foot mega-trophy was created, and each year the winner's name would be engraved on it.

Hot Rod and other rod and custom magazines were impressed with Slonaker's idea, and through the magazines, they informed the hot rodders about the show and roadster competition. The 1950 show was a big success, and the first winner of the "America's Most Beautiful Roadster" award was William Niekamp's blue 1929 Ford roadster, with a track nose. To have enough roadsters at the show, Al Slonaker brought in more than 30 dirt track "hot rod racers," and the rest were local hot rods from the Bay Area and Southern California. There were more than 100 cars in the show this first year, and nearly 28,000 people came to see them.

The "Emperor" won the AMBR award in 1960 and was built by George Barris, Charles Krikorian, Blackie Gejeian, and Richard Peters. The owner was Krikorian, and his '29 roadster had a fully chromed chassis and a one-off grill shell. Today Blackie Gejeian owns it, and the restored former roadster winner was at the 50th show at the Cow Palace in San Francisco. *Michael Dobrin*

In 1951, Wally Parks brought the NHRA Safety Safari to the second National Roadster Show. Joining Parks were four troopers from the California Highway Patrol. *Greg Sharp*

Pretty soon, Al Slonaker's "Grand National Roadster Show" was known as the "Grand Daddy" of the rod and custom shows around the country. The big 9-foot trophy became a part of the feature story when the magazines later published the winning roadster. People from all over the world saw the mega-trophy and the winner in magazines like *Rod & Custom*.

The first time I attended the Oakland Roadster Show was on my trip to the United States in 1969. Like so many other European hot rodders, I had read about it in magazines like *Hot Rod* and *Rod & Custom*, and it was among the first things I wanted to see in America. I was also there to take some pictures for one of the Swedish magazines and was introduced to Al Slonaker, who took me around the show. In 1967 the event had moved to the new Oakland Coliseum, which is where it was held on my first visit. That year Art Himsl won the AMBR (America's Most Beautiful Roadster) with his "Experimental Roadster" called "Alien," and high street machines were the "in" thing. Early '60s Chevies with tube front axles and Model-A Ford springs made them so high that the owners needed ladders to get into their cars. They called them "street funny cars." The show was big even in those days, and its advertising invited all to "come back Sunday night and see 300 roadsters drive out of the show." Although there were some show cars at Oakland, all the hot rods had to run under their own power, in and out of the show, so people lined up outside to see them drive out. The size of the show and all the running hot rods were like magic to this Scandinavian, because at the car shows back home, you could see no more than 10 hot rods at a time.

There have always been plenty of traditional hot rods at the Oakland Show, and most of the well-known hot rodders have had their cars in the show through the years. The one who has had more cars in the show than anyone is Tom Prufer. To date he has had nearly 30 cars in the show during the past 40 years, which must be a record for one person. He started with race cars and dragsters between 1958 and 1964 but returned to hot rod roadsters and coupes. His traditional hot rods always have "Tommy the Greek"–type pinstriping or flames, plus plenty of louvers and loud pipes. He has never won the AMBR, but was close once with a '29 high-boy roadster.

The guy who has the most wins of the big trophy is Ernie Immerso, with three. He won in 1988 with his Ardun-powered '32 roadster, and in 1989 with the "Golden Star" 25 T. He came back with the Ford Indy DOHC-powered V-8 T to win again in 1991. The car builder with the most wins is Boyd Coddington, who has had six winners between 1982 and 1999. Coddington also set the standard for winners in the future, and during the 1994 show that standard was right in the spotlight when Joe McPherson's Infinity-powered '29 track roadster

George Barris was at all the big shows of the '50s and '60s, and in between he was building new winners. This '27 T-roadster on a '32 frame was named "Twister-T," and he painted it in a Peacock Metalflake. The car won the AMBR in 1962, and in 1998 it was restored for exhibition at the 50th show. Dual headlights were featured on many of Barris' cars during the late '50s and early '60s. *Michael Dobrin*

Tall T creations took some strange forms in the '60s, and one of them was Steve and George Scott's "roadster" with a tall top. The engine was a fuel-injected Buick Nailhead. Los Angeles was the brothers' hometown, but they toured the car around the country and won trophies at many shows. *Michael Dobrin*

went up against Boyd's "Roadstar." The Chip Foose–designed, fenderless, '36 Ford-type roadster that was built for Buz De Vosta had a Caddy Northstar engine in the rear. With those two expensive cars, the question became, "Would it now take a $250,000–$350,000 roadster to win the AMBR trophy?" Since then, a few roadsters have won without the owners having spent that kind of money on their cars. But winning the AMBR with a low-budget, homemade roadster is not possible today.

During the last 20 years most of the AMBR winners have been high-tech–style roadsters, but with the new nostalgia wave in rod building, a new trophy had to be created. It was collector Bruce Meyer who came up with the idea and created "The Bruce Meyer Hot Rod Preservation Perpetual Trophy." This award will ensure that the best pre-1955 nostalgia hot rod in the show will get a very prestigious trophy. The first year for that trophy was in 1997, and Gary Scroeder and Rick Creese won with their

*H*ot Rod magazine supported the first National Roadster Show in 1950, and at the 50th show they recreated one of the most famous covers of the magazine. The May 1952 issue featured Dick Flint's '29 Ford roadster on the cover. Joe Sievers' clone of the Flint roadster is pictured in the previous chapter.

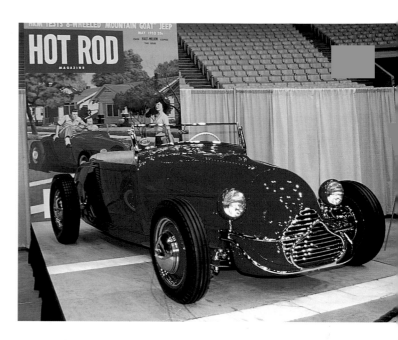

1927 T-roadster. In 1998 it was Tommy Classon, all the way from Eskilstuna, Sweden, who won with his flathead-powered '32 roadster. (See chapter 4.) It was a long and costly trip for Tommy, but to win the Meyer award was a big deal for the Swede.

The 1999 and 50th show was held at the Cow Palace in San Francisco. The three halls were filled with hot rods and customs, and the main hall was for roadsters only. This was the show to remember, and with about 450 cars, it took days to see everything. The big winner of the year was Fred Warren, with his new Chip Foose–designed '33-style high-tech roadster. The project was started at

*B*lackie Gejeian did not win the AMBR in 1953 when he entered the show with his black '27 T. The roadster has been parked in his garage for more than 40 years, but it was restored just in time for the big 50th show. Gejeian chromed nearly all the chassis parts and most of the pieces on the 296-ci tuned flathead motor.

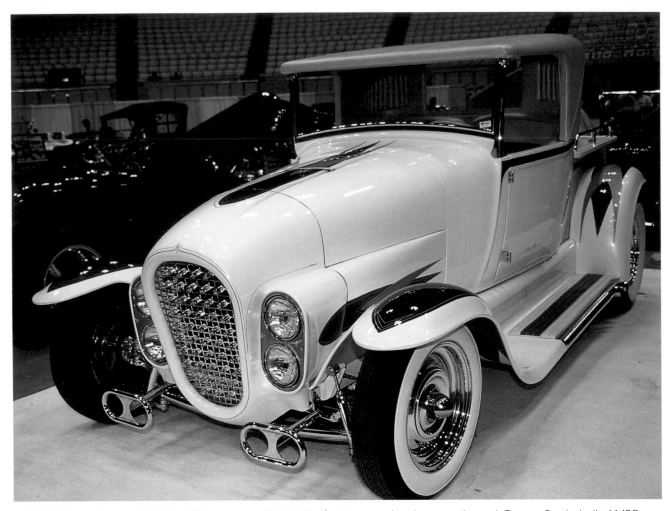

This is not the real "Ala Kart." You can see that in the front suspension, because the real George Barris–built AMBR winner has coil springs and airbags in front of the axle. It was Howdy Ledbetter who built this nice replica for the 1996 show, and he finished it on the day the show opened. Ledbetter called it "The"Howli Kart," after his daughter.

Hot Rods by Boyd, where Larry Sergejeff did the chassis and Marcel's fabricated the handmade steel body before Boyd closed the shop. When three of the boys from Boyd's started to work for Chuck Lombardo's California Street Rods, Warren let that shop take over and finish the new car. It paid off, too, and won the AMBR award.

There were many good-looking nostalgia cars at the 50th show, and the car that won the Bruce Meyer

This old-style chopped and channeled '32 Ford pickup came all the way from New York for the 50th show. The owner and builder is Gary Chopit from the Chopit Kustom Shop in Hicksville, N.Y. With a last name like that, you must have something wild to drive, and the truck has a small-block Chevy with six carburetors on a log manifold. Today's air suspension makes it possible to drive it too.

The George Barris "Twister-T" was an AMBR winner in 1962, and it was restored for the 50th show. This DeSoto hemi-powered T on a '32 chassis was featured in many TV shows during the '60s, and the green metalflake paint is very bright against the white interior and whitewall tires.

Bruce Meyers has saved many important cars of hot rod history; one of them is Frank Mack's '27 track roadster. The car is still unrestored but in pretty good shape. There is a tuned flathead under the hood. In the background is the first winner of the AMBR award, the Niekamp '29 roadster, which Jake Jacobs owns today.

There are also many nice nostalgia hot rods on the East Coast, and Mike Mann's blue '32 roadster is one of those entered in the 50th show. It has all the old goodies like a Halibrand rear end, frame with Model A cross-members, '52 Mercury flathead with an Isky cam, Edelbrock heads, and "slingshot" manifold.

When *Hot Rod* magazine was ready to celebrate 50 years in the business, it needed a hot rod as a symbol. Regg Schlemmer owned the '27 track roadster that was on the cover of the first issue of *Hot Rod* in January 1948, and they had Roy Brizio Street Rods build a replica of that car. This new version has a Wescott replica body and a 302 Ford motor. The car was on the cover of the January 1998 issue of *Hot Rod* and appeared at the Oakland show the same year.

Award in 1999 was Ken Gross' "black & basic" '32 flathead-powered roadster. This steel roadster has all the right parts, including a 304-inch late-model flathead with Scot blower and Eddie Meyer heads. There is also a Lincoln-geared '39 Ford transmission behind the hot flat-motor, and a Halibrand rear end. Dave Simard at East Coast Customs built this black beauty. Under the Carson-style top, you can find a saddle-tan leather interior by Steve Pierce. There were other roadsters that could have won the Meyer award, too, like the red McGee '32

One must call him "Mr. Oakland Roadster Show," because Tom Prufer has had more cars in the show than any other private hot rodder: nearly 30 cars in 40 years, and his latest is this red '32 coupe with flames. A typical "100 Pruf" hot rod has plenty of louvers, flames, and loud pipes, is chopped and has a "kick-ass motor." His "flame-man," Rod Powell, did the flames as always, and the only unusual thing on the new coupe is the painted Halibrand wheels.

Ken Gross runs the Petersen Automotive Museum in L.A., and he has this time-perfect '32 roadster built by Dave Simard at East Coast Customs. The steel roadster has a big, full race 304 flathead under the hood, with a SCOT supercharger, Eddie Meyer heads, and Harman & Collins magneto. Gross won the Bruce Meyer Award at the 50th show.

S ven Sandberg from Stockholm, Sweden, built his "Glowing Coupe" in 1961. When he bought it back in the early '90s it was impossible to restore. He used what parts he could and replaced the rest of them with replica parts. The body is now fiberglass, but the chopped and channeled '32 coupe still looks the same. The car was shipped to the '98 Roadster Show.

roadster restored by So-Cal Speed Shop in time for the show. The only problem was that Bruce Meyer owns that car, and it might look like a conflict of interest if he won the prize that bears his name. The other contender was Mike Mann's East Coast Steel '32 roadster with a light-blue paint job, and a fully tuned '52 Mercury flathead. The National Roadster Show is the place to be if you want to see the best of both the old and the new in hot rodding.

Just the color of this '29 high boy on '32 rails will make you look closer at it. This roadster was built by Rich Guasco and won the AMBR award in 1951. The same owner still has the car, and it is now restored, with a 327 Chevy engine under the hood and a four-speed transmission. Rick Valdez painted the car and Custom Concept Interiors did the upholstery.

Chapter 8

HOT ROD EVENTS AND RUNS

To live in California is nearly too much of a good thing when it comes to all of the hot rod events from February to December. The only problem is to pick the right events, because there are so many going on during the season. It starts in February with the Temecula Rod Run, when they fill Temecula's Old Town with a two-day street rod happening. The weather is usually good, with sunshine and temperatures in the 60s–70s. To walk around this little Wild West town, looking at all kinds of street rods, will take nearly a full day. This is the perfect family event, too, because if you don't want to see cars all day, there are all kinds of antique stores, restaurants, and cafés in town. The Temecula run can host thousands of street rods, but it depends on the weather report right before the event.

Not all events have to be that big either, and some Saturday mornings I drive my nostalgia T-roadster to the Donut Shop on Adams in Huntington Beach. Through the years many of the local hot rodders have stopped at the Donut Shop on their way to work, and they go there

This line of classic hot rods is from the Street Rod Nationals in Sweden, and the group is a club called the Prinsbo Outlaws. Five of the six Model A and '32 Fords have tuned flathead engines, and the gold-painted A-roadster has an early hemi motor. The owner of the purple '32 convertible, Micke Fors, builds the nostalgia chassis and Halibrand rear ends that help many nostalgia hot rodders in Scandinavia get their cars together.

Buddy Dughi is one of the boys behind the "Lucky Devils" club, and his '30 Ford coupe has fooled many hot rodders into believing that there is a 409 Chevy in it. The truth is that it is a small-block Chevy, with older 348-409 valve covers. The little coupe has a six-carburetor manifold and whitewall tires on copper-painted steel wheels that match the scalloped body well.

During the past few years, the start of Tom's Fun Run in Placentia, California, begins with all the cars lined up on the street for a group photo. With about 350 cars in seven rows, you need some help from the local police to keep the other traffic rolling in the neighborhood.

Track roadsters are getting very popular again, and if you cannot find an old one with some history, you can create your own, as did Marty Strode of Cornelius, Oregon. He built his own frame from 4x2-inch tubing and used a fiberglass replica body. The engine is a 276-ci '53 Mercury with three 97 Stromberg carbs. With some old pictures and much hard work, you can create a piece of history like this.

Many new-generation clubs drive their primed early-style hot rods to the yearly West Coast Kustoms event in Paso Robles, California, the last weekend of May. The '24 steel-bodied T-roadster belongs to Kevan Sledge and has a 331 '49 Caddy motor with a Howard cam plus a four-carb manifold.

every Saturday morning to have a cup of java and talk to their friends. This goes on all year, and most Saturday mornings there are about 200 cars in the parking lot. You can always see some neat, basic hot rods there.

Swap meets are also a very good place to see some old-time hot rods. One of my favorites, the monthly swap meet at Veterans Stadium in Long Beach, is one of the best places to find parts, meet people, and see some nice cars. But the best swap meet of the year is the Big-3 at Qualcomm (formerly Jack Murphy) Stadium, San Diego, the last weekend in February. There you can still find most of the old parts, even if some are on the expensive side. There are hundreds of cars for sale, and it will take you a full day of walking if you like to check out all the parts for sale. If you can't find what you're looking for in parts, you can at least get some good connections to help you find them later.

A rod run that is something to look forward to every spring is "Tom's Fun Run," founded many years ago by Tom McMullen and now sponsored by *Street Rodder* magazine. The unique thing

Paul Bragg is a well-known body man and customizer in Northern California, and most of the cars he has driven to the Paso Robles event during the past 5–10 years are customs. But this time he built himself a very nice '32 five-window coupe with an early hemi for power. This type of nostalgic chopped and channeled coupe is becoming popular again. With a set of old-type whitewall tires, it will look like a real '50s hot rod.

about this run is that the stops are mainly at street rod–related companies in Orange County, and the final stop is always with lunch at a nice park somewhere.

If you want to see a mix of street rods and street machines, the GoodGuys have two events a year at the Pomona Fairplex: the So-Cal Nationals, with cars up to 1964 in mid-May; and the West Coast Hot Rod Happening the last weekend of July. For people in Northern California, there are two big events at the Pleasanton Fairgrounds: the All-American Get-Together the last weekend of March, and the huge West Coast Nationals at the end of August.

Another great place to see classic hot rods is the West Coast Kustoms event in Paso Robles, California, during Memorial Day weekend each May. The little town of Paso Robles is filled with neat customs and hot rods. The three-day event offers crusin' Friday night and a big show in the park in the middle of town Saturday and Sunday. This event is also one of the places where you can see many of the new generation hot rodders with their basic and old-style hot rods in primer. They come from all over the West Coast to have a fun weekend in Paso.

The Muroc Reunion and the lakes racing at Edwards Air Force Base are also places to see many old-style hot rods, and see them run. This is also a

Tom Branch from San Gabriel, California, is one of the younger hot rodders and a member of the Auto Butchers club. He found this old '29 roadster for sale and restored it. Today it has a small-block Chevy with three carburetors, but it is easy to guess that it was built with a flathead or an early Caddy or Olds engine. The body was not just channeled; the doors were welded shut, too.

favorite event for all the older generation hot rodders on the West Coast, and some of them still have their cars running. For this event you can count on two things: it will be hot, and you will see many well-known hot rodders and some of their cars. Guys like Wally Parks, the Pierson Brothers, Bruce Meyer, Pete Chapouris, P-Wood, and many more will be there to check out all the cool hot rods and maybe even run their cars on the track just for fun. There might be as many as 400 nostalgia cars out there, so it is definitely an event that you should not miss.

If you like the early, early hot rods, the Antique

Nationals at L.A. Raceway in Palmdale, California, is for you. There, you'll find Model Ts, tuned Model As and old-style dragsters with tuned flatheads, or Ardun flatheads for power. The Four-Forever club shows off its stuff and runs at the race track, too.

Next page
The annual Orange County Outriders' picnic is at Irwin Lake, and with about 300 cars in the park, this is a popular event. To make the members happy, the club has plenty of good food and a live band playing all afternoon.

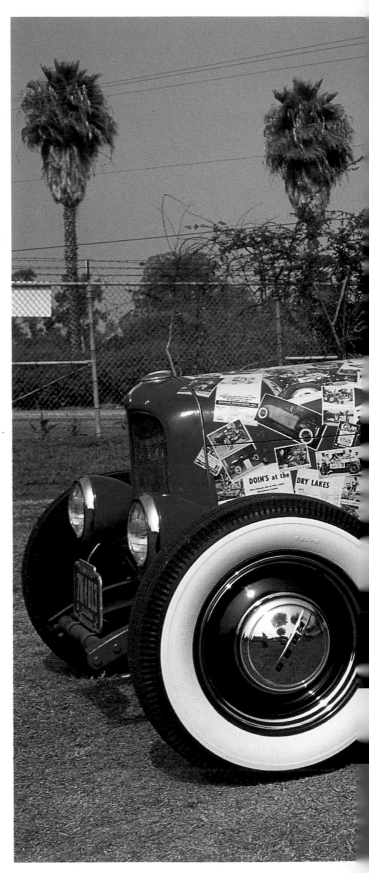

Doug Lindow is a flathead man who builds flat motors for his friends, and he always wanted a '28–29 highboy roadster. With all the replica parts of today, he could build a new car with the late '40s–early '50s look. The frame is built with American Stamping rails, and the body is a new steel replica made by Brookville. Under the hood is a 59AB flathead with two Ford carburetors on an Eddie Meyer manifold, and a set of Meyer heads.

Pete Chapouris keeps busy running his So-Cal Speed Shop, but he takes time off for Tom's Fun Run in this little green '27 roadster that he built for his dad years ago. It has a Ford V-6 engine under the Steve Davis–made aluminum hood. The '36 coupe in the background is also a Chapouris-built car, built for Billy Gibbons of ZZ Top.

Jim "Jake" Jacobs has been Pete Chapouris' business partner for about 30 years, but now and then he shows us how to get back to basics when it comes to hot rods. His '28 Ford Phaeton was built in 28 days and then painted with a brush at the West Coast Nationals. When he and Tony Thacker glued all the pictures from old hot rod magazines on the body of the '29, it was published even more.

This Model A modified was built by Dave Lukkari from Apple Valley, California, and it has all the right parts. The engine is a flathead with Ardun heads and a blower on top with two Stromberg carburetors. He built his roadster with a front half of a Phaeton body and a frame with a "suicide" front end and a Halibrand rear end. Dave drives his roadster everywhere. This picture shows it at the NHRA Reunion in Bakersfield.

What many hot rodders here in Southern California consider to be *the* event of the year is the L.A. Roadsters' Fathers Day meeting at the Pomona Fairplex. It has hundreds of roadsters, both high-tech and nostalgia, and a swap meet with all the old stuff for sale.

One of the older clubs in the Orange County area is the "Outriders," and they have their yearly event in September. In recent years, they have held the annual picnic at Irvine Lake, in Irvine, which is a neat place to have a street rod event that time of the year.

Another "must" for a nostalgia hot rodder is the NHRA Hot Rod Reunion at Famoso Raceway in Bakersfield. Drag racing has been a big part of the hot rodding history, and this event includes all types of old dragsters and hot rods. At the reunion, the NHRA inducts members into its Hall of Fame, so you have a chance to see some famous personalities of years past. This event is also a favorite of the new clubs and their members, so in the pits you will see primed Model-A high-boy roadsters, low-channeled coupes, and

Collector Bruce Meyer has many famous old hot rods, and most of them were restored by So-Cal Speed Shop. This three-window '32 Ford with chopped top and a blown Ardun is one of his "drivers," but it is so nice that he took it to the Oakland Roadster Show in 1998.

plenty of old-style club jackets. Names like Shifters, Choppers, Auto Butchers, and Lucky Devils can be seen all over the place. The reunion is in November. Just before Christmas, Mark Morton and his friends in the River City Rodders host the Reliability Run the first weekend of December. This run begins at a parking lot in Riverside, with morning coffee and donuts. At 8 A.M. sharp the first car takes off on a three-to-four-hour run up in the mountains, with a stop for lunch at the end of the course. Neat cars and good scenery are things that you will see a lot of on the Reliability Run.

Rock 'n' roll and hot rods go together. One famous rock guitarist and bandleader who owns both hot rods and customs is Brian Setzer, with his Stray Cats jacket on. Here he is checking out a '29 flathead high boy at the GoodGuys event in Pomona.

CLASSIC HOT ROD REPLICAS OF TODAY

Many of us hot rodders want that special classic hot rod that is impossible to buy today. Thanks to its history, it has become far too expensive, and the owner might not even want to sell it for all the gold in California. How many enthusiasts didn't want a yellow '32 "Graffiti Coupe" after seeing John Milner drive one in *American Graffiti*? Or a ZZ Top '33 "Eliminator" Coupe? Replica parts make it possible to build "new" old hot rods again, and without spending too much money.

The first reproduction component introduced on the market was the T-bucket kit, with a fiberglass body and a square tubing frame. They have sold this

The So-Cal Speed Shop roadster was one of the most important new hot rods of 1998, and Jake Jacobs created a full series of parts for it. It was a very hot day in August when I took the pictures, so I enjoyed going for a breezy spin with Chapouris in the roadster. I was very impressed with how smooth the ride was, especially over the railroad tracks. When the plan came up to change the name of the PC3G over to So-Cal Speed Shop there was also a new roadster on the drawing table. The car was going to be built for Alex Xydias, who started So-Cal Speed Shop in 1946, and also as a symbol of the new series of nostalgia parts that were being created. They built the roadster with replica components, like the Brookville steel body and Halibrand "kidney bean" style wheels by PS Engineering.

The So-Cal crew also wanted a brown leather interior over the special folding seat. Ron Mangus did the stitching. The restored steering wheel is from a '40 Ford, and the dash has a full set of vintage Moon gauges in a So-Cal dash insert. Check out the door straps with the So-Cal logo.

Fresh horsepower was needed under the hood, so a 390-horsepower 355-ci Chevy small-block was built by Motor X in Oklahoma City. The engine has 9.2:1 compression, Edelbrock manifold, RPM heads, and a Carter/Weber carburetor. The engine has the torque curve perfect for a hot rod roadster with an automatic transmission, and that is one of the secrets of the smooth ride of the car.

It took Joe Sievers in Vincennes, Indiana, 16 years to build this perfect replica of the famous Dick Flint roadster. It was in 1952 that the real roadster was on the cover of *Hot Rod*, and it took nearly 30 years before Sievers got started on his project. He dropped the frame and channeled the steel '29 roadster body just like the original to get the right look. The front end has a hand-formed aluminum nose and hood made by Sievers.

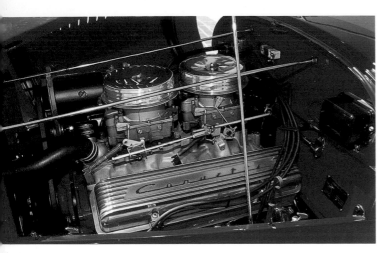

Originally, Dick Flint had a tuned '40 Mercury flathead under the hood, but in 1960 he swapped that for a '57 Chevy Corvette 283 Chevy with dual four-barrel carburetors. He bolted the motor to the '39 Ford transmission with the help of an adapter. When Sievers built his version of the Flint roadster, he got hold of a '57 Corvette engine, and dropped that in the car. Every detail on the engine is exactly like it was in 1960.

inexpensive type of kit car since the '60s. Next came the replica Model A and '32 roadster bodies that gave many rodders a new chance to build their dream cars. When original '32 Ford chassis became hard to find, and good frames even harder, Roy Fjastad at Deuce Factory solved the problem by starting to produce just-like-stock, stamped-out '32 Ford frame rails. Since then, different companies have produced thousands of '32 frame rails.

The most-copied T-buckets are Tommy Ivo's and Norm Grabowski's, already discussed in chapter 1. The T-bucket kits they sold in the '60s and '70s were based on those two early hot rods. Through the years the kits have changed a little bit, but basically they still build them like the Grabowski and Ivo Ts. The kits have used rear ends like 8–9-inch Fords and independent Jaguars with coil-over shocks, instead of the '40 Ford with a leaf spring. By the time the kits came out on the market, the most common engine was the small-block Chevy, instead of the early Caddy and Buick engines.

It did not take long before the Model-A kits and parts became available on the market, but the early

Busby doesn't keep his Flint replica locked up in his garage, but takes it out for a spin to the local hot rod events now and then. It is an amazing little roadster that makes people stop and scrutinize the great detail work. The early dirt track tires were not easy to find when Sievers was building the car, but he found a set of ribbed fronts, and the rears are 7.50x16 Firestones.

The most-copied hot rod of them all is the John Milner "Graffiti Coupe" shown at hot rod events around the world. Some are perfect replicas, like this one that Roy Fjastad Jr. built for a customer in Japan. The customer, Shun, bought the five-window body already chopped, but it still took weeks of metal work before it could be lifted on the Fjastad chassis. The modern tires are one of the few things that are different from the original. Roy is an active hot rod builder with his Deuce Ranch Company, and he has some help from the rest of the Fjastad family. His brother, Carl, owns the Deuce Frame Company and does the basic chassis work, then most of the components come from his other brother, Jay, who runs The Deuce Factory.

Just like in the original "Graffiti Coupe," Roy used a Man-A-Free manifold, with four carburetors, on top of the small-block Chevy engine. Cal Custom valve covers were also a part of the look that he wanted. Some of the parts are not that easy to find anymore, so it took Roy some time on the phone to locate the right stuff.

fiberglass roadster bodies were very simple. They were a one-piece shell, and you had to cut the door openings, fiberglass-in a plywood floor, and put in the hours to make it a functional body. Today, people value their time, so they want a body that is ready to bolt onto the chassis. "Time is money," so people pay more for the body but get the car rolling sooner.

In the early days of replicas, only roadster bodies were available, but today there are nearly all models, including coupes, sedans, roadster pickups, and Phaetons. Many builders realize that even if you find a real steel body for sale, it will take many hours at the body shop just to straighten it out and get it ready for paint. If you want a coupe chopped, that job alone would cost you nearly as much as buying a chopped and ready fiberglass coupe body. Therefore, many hot rodders take the easy way out and buy a fiberglass replica, while others do it the hard way and buy a real steel body.

During the decade, pieces and complete steel replica bodies have been made by a couple of companies in the United States. The body styles were mostly open Model As, but later the '34 roadster and convertible became available. For years, different companies said they planned to make the body all the hot rodders were waiting for—the '32 Ford roadster. Some manufacturers started to accept payments for bodies, but no bodies materialized. It took until 1997 before Brookville showed off their new steel roadster body, and soon the first bodies were delivered to hot rod shops throughout the country. The first body was delivered in pieces to So-Cal Speed Shop in Pomona, California, where they had a plan for it already. Pete Chapouris and his team at So-Cal created a full line of nostalgia parts for the '32 roadster they were building for the shop's founder, Alex Xydias. Jake Jacobs designed most of the chassis parts, and he came up with a new way to box the '32 frame rails. He moved the box-plates inside the rails and called it "step-boxing." It gives you more room for fuel and brake lines and such.

Brookville's goal for the new chassis was to offer nostalgic style and simple build-up, but good handling. There are different setups to choose from, but the basic is a dropped front axle with leaf spring, hairpins, and a panhard bar to keep it from rolling sideways on the spring. The rear end can be either a Halibrand Quick change or a Ford 8-9 inches with long ladder-bars and a leaf-spring or coil-overs. The frame is also set up for a small-block Chevy and TH 350-400 or 700 automatic transmissions.

The first roadster with the replica steel Brookville body was built for Alex Xydias, but also to be the symbol for the new era of the So-Cal Speed Shop. I had a chance to go for a spin in the new roadster, and it is the best "leaf-spring rod" I have ever ridden. It combines today's technology with the old look, and now the So-Cal team is building about three of

A second-generation street rod builder who is making many dreams come true is Roy Brizio of San Francisco. He builds more than 10 cars a year, and this project started as a '50s-style Neal East full-fendered roadster. Ford was part of the project from the beginning, so the roadster received a new small-block 302 Ford engine and a five-speed transmission. To get the right lines on the car, the grill shell was cut down 2 inches, giving the hood a little bit of a rake.

124

The white tuck 'n' roll interior was a perfect match for the purple DuPont metallic paint, and the dash of the Wescott fiberglass body was filled with a set of Ford gauges in an old-style Lobeck insert. The steering column was made by Mullins, and the steering wheel is a Bell replica.

those chassis a week. Some customers have ordered copies of the So-Cal roadsters, which feature the same look but with different colors of paint.

With all the replica parts for '32 Fords on the market, there are many more '32 roadsters out there today than the 15,000 that Ford originally manufactured. Some hot rodders focus in on a very special historical hot rod, many times a car featured in the hot rod magazines of the 1950s. With all the published pictures available, it is possible to recreate a replica that is close enough to the original to fool most anybody. The Dick Flint roadster is one of those famous and much-published hot rods for

which many hot rodders would give an arm and a leg. Joe Sievers was one hot rodder who did something about it, and it took him 16 years to collect all the parts for an exact replica of his favorite hot rod. Not long after the car was finished, Siever sold it to Jim Busby in Newport Beach, California. The real Flint roadster, owned by the collector Don Orosco, is also restored, but it has the flathead under the hood. The replica was built just like Flint's car was in the late '50s and early '60s, with a '57 Corvette 283 Chevy engine under the hood, perhaps so there would be a difference between the two roadsters.

One of the very busy street rod builders that

A big part of the look on a hot rod is the wheels, and Roy Brizio picked a set of chromed steel wheels with big whitewall tires and '50 Mercury hubcaps. The dropped front end, big white "donuts," and the purple metallic paint made for a very nice combination on this roadster, which Roy Brizio drove to the Street Rod Nationals and many other long distance runs.

makes mostly replicas is Roy Brizio Street Rods in San Francisco. One of the projects that I took a closer look at was Roy's own full-fendered '32 roadster, which was going to be a real "driver." Thom Taylor did the design, and the look is an early '60s Neal East–style roadster. Not just another "Deuce-roadster," it was built on a new '32 frame with a leaf-spring front suspension and a coil-over rear-suspended 9-inch Ford rear end. The engine is a 300+ horsepower 302 SVO Ford motor with dual carburetors, and behind it is a five-speed transmission.

To get the right look, Roy dropped the grill shell 2 inches, and that made the lines of the hood

perfect. But it did mean that the bead on the body had to be modified to fit the new hood line. That was easier to do with the Wescott replica fiberglass body. Big whitewall tires on chromed steel wheels, with '50 Mercury hubcaps, contrasted nicely against the purple DuPont metallic paint and white tuck and roll interior.

Building replica hot rods is the wave of the future, because we cannot count on having the luxury of the old Ford bodies 20 to 25 years from now. Still, I bet that an early-style '32 roadster will be as popular then as it has been during the last 50 years.

INDEX